ADJUSTMENT PROBLEMS OF AFRICAN STUDENTS AT PUBLIC UNIVERSITIES IN AMERICA

Apollos Bitrus Goyol

Edited by Sheila K. Dodson

University Press of America,® Inc.
Lanham · Boulder · New York · Toronto · Oxford

Copyright © 2006 by
University Press of America,® Inc.
4501 Forbes Boulevard
Suite 200
Lanham, Maryland 20706
UPA Acquisitions Department (301) 459-3366

PO Box 317
Oxford
OX2 9RU, UK

Library of Congress Control Number: 2006921391
ISBN-13: 978-0-7618-2983-6 (paperback : alk. paper)
ISBN-10: 0-7618-2983-0 (paperback : alk. paper)

⊖™ The paper used in this publication meets the minimum
requirements of American National Standard for Information
Sciences—Permanence of Paper for Printed Library Materials,
ANSI Z39.48—1984

Table of Contents

Figures

Preface

More international students are enrolled in colleges and universities in the United States (US) than in any other country, as reported by the Institute of International Education. Open Doors reports that international students contribute nearly $12 billion in money spent on tuition, living expenses, and related costs. Nearly 75% of funding for all international students comes from personal and family resources or other sources outside of the US. The Department of Commerce data describe US higher education as the country's fifth largest service sector export. In the 2002–2003 school year, the Institute estimated that 586,323 international students were studying in the US. Approximately 302,058 (52%) of these students came from countries in Asia, and 80,584 (13.7%) came from Europe. Latin America had the third largest representation with 63,634 (10.8%) students, followed by the Middle East with 36,858 (6.3%), Africa with 34,217 (5.8%), North America with 25,888 (4.4 %) , and Oceania with 4,624 (0.8%). Only 10 (1.71%) students were unidentified by country. As a response to the high number of international students, an increasing amount of literature has addressed the specific needs, unique experiences, and acculturation patterns of these students (Essandoh, 1995; Hayes & Lin, 1994; Pedersen, 1991; Sandhu, 1995).

Adjustment is defined as the process through which individuals become integrated into a new environment, including the satisfaction of motivations and needs. Adjustment/acculturation research on international students has revealed that variables such as perceived discrimination, use of the English language, finances, and shorter time spent in the US contribute to lower levels of adjustment. The impact of declared majors, length of stay, marital status, age, and gender in the adjustment process has also been addressed in several studies, revealing conflicting results.

Therefore, the main objective of this book is to take a critical look at the adjustment problems as experienced by African students at public universities in America and to provide these students with information that will result in smooth transitions into the American academic community. The increase in pluralism and cultural diversity in the US has been markedly reflected in its educational systems (Institute of International Education, 2002). According to Thomas and Althen (1989), international students share certain characteristics regardless of their diverse cultural, social, religious, and political backgrounds. For instance, unlike other ethnic minorities, refugees, or recent immigrants, most international students plan to return to their home countries eventually and are in the US only temporarily. They are people in transition who choose to live in a foreign academic setting to realize their educational objectives. Because they are far away from their immediate families, other relatives, and friends, they are also likely to have basic social support networks that are very distinctive from those of American students. Faced with a new set of basic values and beliefs, international students are continually challenged to accommodate themselves to a variety of acculturation and adjustment problems (Berry, 1980).

For the international student, your ultimate goal for coming to America is to achieve in academics. Therefore, the primary objective of this book is to present you with realistic and practical information that will make your academic venture to America a successful and memorable experience. I sincerely believe that many of you are highly self-motivated and are motivated for your families and for the prestige of achieving academically in an American university setting. The potential impact of your studying in this country is not quantifiable. At best, it can only be imagined, because among you will be political leaders, scientists, and researchers. The intellectual strength of many countries from the African continent and the parameter for measuring your success is your ability to translate functional education into a socially useful instrument of scientific, economic, educational, political, and technological transformation. Congratulations and welcome to your various campuses.

Acknowledgements

First, I would like to thank the Lord God Almighty, without whom this book would be possible, for bringing me this far.

To Western Michigan University and in particular the College of Education and International Student and Scholars Services office for believing in me and equipping me for life. Thank you so much.

To University Press of America, Inc, thank you so much for giving me this unique opportunity to publish this book.

To my children, Wadelnen and Nenfot, and especially my dear wife, Jemima, for your prayers, support, encouragement, understanding, and patience, all of which gave me the strength to go on. May the good Lord continuously bless you as we all look forward to the future with lots optimism according to His will.

In addition, I would like to thank Sheila K. Dodson for her editorial support during the preparation of this book.

Finally, I dedicate this work to my dear parents for all their relentless prayers and unwavering support.

Chapter I. Introduction

The Institute of International Education (2004) reports that more international students are enrolled in colleges and universities in the United States (US) than in any other country. For the 2002–2003 school year, the Institute estimated that 586,323 international students were studying in the US. Approximately 302,058 (52%) came from countries in Asia, and 80,584 (13.7%) came from Europe. Latin America had the third largest representation with 63,634 (10.8%), followed by the Middle East with 36,858 (6.3%), Africa with 34,217 (5.8%), North America with 25,888 (4.4%), and Oceania with 4,624 (0.8%). Only 10 (1.71%) students were unidentified by country. Concomitant with the high number of international students, an increasing amount of literature has addressed the specific needs, unique experiences, and acculturation patterns of these students (Essandoh, 1995; Hayes & Lin, 1994; Pedersen, 1991; Sandhu, 1995).

In recent years, adjustment to American culture by international students has been viewed from an acculturation perspective, although international students do not hold a "normal" minority status (Berry, 1980). A common definition of an international student is "anyone who is enrolled in courses at institutions of higher education in the US who is not a US citizen, an immigrant (permanent resident), or a refugee" (Institute of International Education, 2002). As early as 1955, Lysgaard suggested, based on self-reports of attitudes toward their host country after completing programs of various lengths in the US, a U-curve exists in the adjustment pattern of international students. Specifically, there is a general positive attitude toward the host country for those returning home after 6 months, a negative and critical attitude for students returning home after 1 year, and a positive attitude again for students who returned home after 18 months. Similar patterns of adjustment were also identified for international students who remained in the US (i.e., longitudinally, at 6, 12, and 18 months). The U-curve hypothesis can be related to the adjustment pattern that international students go through as shown in the adjustment cycle figure. At the start of the sojourn, the international student is likely to be excited by finally arriving in the US and generally feels optimistic toward the host country. However, soon the reality of academic work in a foreign language, difficulty developing close friendships, and the hassles of everyday tasks all combine to generate feelings of frustration, self-doubt, and negative attitudes toward the host country and its educational system. Gradually, as the student gains in the requisite understanding and competencies for successfully meeting the challenges of the host country's social and educational environment, finds a few friends, etc., that student's self-esteem, general attitude, and emotions tend to improve. This upward turning phase is enhanced by the prospect of returning home, especially for those students who have impending bright futures (Institute of International Education, 1994; Sewell & Davidson, 1956).

The theory of acculturation focuses on understanding the adaptation processes and cultural changes of minority groups as they experience firsthand contact with a dominant culture (Sodowsky, Lai, & Plake, 1991; Sodowsky & Plake, 1992). Originally, acculturation was defined as a process of cultural change that occurred at a group level (Redfield, Linton, & Herskovits, 1936). Today, it is also recognized as attitudinal and behavioral changes in an individual whose cultural group is mutually experiencing acculturation (Berry, Kim, Minde, & Mok, 1987; Graves, 1967; Moyerman & Forman, 1992).

Although there are many models of acculturation, one of the most well known models is the Bidirectional Acculturation Model (Berry, 1980; 1983). This model proposes that a minority person's psychological adjustment to a new culture can occur in four different ways: (1) integration, (2) assimilation, (3) rejection, and (4) deculturation. *Integration* refers to a person's desire to belong to the majority culture, whereas *assimilation* refers to the extent to which a person feels he or she has acculturated into the majority culture at the expense of his or her own culture. *Rejection* is defined as the tendency to reject the majority culture to maintain one's native culture. Finally, *deculturation* reflects the extent to which a person feels that he or she cannot identify with either the native or the majority culture. Differences that distinguish one culture from others are what provide individuals of the first culture with a unique sense of cultural identity. These differences are impossible to replicate in a foreign country. Therefore, the loss of cultural objects such as the symbolism of the national flag, music, and art, as well as numerous other background aspects of the home culture, can have a significant impact on the international student's quality of adjustment in the new environment.

The acculturating process is considered a difficult, reactive, and conflicting process, rather than a smooth transition. The process is difficult and reactive because it involves the adjustment of a minority group, or a minority person, to the culture of a dominant group (Berry, 1983). Stress is often experienced during the acculturation process (acculturative stress) and takes the form of anxiety, depression, identity confusion, feelings of alienation, and heightened psychosomatic symptom levels (Berry et al., 1987). As international students leave their home environment, they lose a familiar support system (Essandoh, 1995). Pedersen (1991) suggested that loss of a support system could result in increased anxiety and loss of self-esteem.

Understanding American behavior and adjusting to it may be a difficult task for international students (Sandhu, 1995). Winkelman (1994) noted that socialization in a new culture is not a continuation of the development process that began in the home country. Many factors come into play. First, the student's legal status as an alien may imply to his native peers that he is transient in American society and brand him from the beginning as an outsider. In addition, as a foreigner, the international student may not have a clear idea of what is expected of him or her. Culture shock is another common experience among international students after their arrival in the US (Ozbay, 1984; Sandhu, 1995; Sandhu & Asrabadi, 1994; Spradley & Phillips, 1972). According to Winkelman (1994), the resolution of culture shock lies in learning how to make an acceptable adaptation to the new culture. There may be an adjustment without adaptation, such as "flight" or isolation. Many people who go to foreign countries do not effectively adapt; instead, they choose to return home during the crises phase. Others use various forms of isolation, for example, living in an ethnic enclave and avoiding substantial learning about the new culture, which slows the acculturation process (Mori, 2000). If the international student desires to function effectively, however, then it is necessary to adjust and adapt. Gradually, the international student makes new friends, increases his self-esteem and general attitude, and gains the requisite understanding and competencies for successfully meeting the challenges of the host country's social and educational environment. The student begins to develop problem-solving skills for dealing with the culture and begins to accept the culture's way with a positive attitude. The culture begins to make sense, and negative reactions and responses to the culture are reduced as one recognizes that problems are due to the inability to understand, accept, and adapt.

All college and university students need to adapt to their new educational and social environments (Ginter & Glauser, 1997). Research has shown that many international students experience a lack of resources and support necessary to deal with various situations, such as cultural and social difficulties (Winkelman, 1994). These students also express a greater need for career and academic advice compared to American students (Cheng, Leong, & Geist, 1993; Day & Hajji, 1986; Heikinheimo & Shute, 1986; Leong & Sedlacek, 1989; Pedersen, 1991). In addition to the adjustment issues that every student has, international students encounter additional stressors due to the demands of cultural adjustments. Linguistic, academic, interpersonal, financial, and intrapersonal problems constitute unique sources of stress (Mori, 2000). Thus, adjustment into American culture and university life can be difficult, causing international students acculturative stress.

Acculturation is desirable for both American and international students. The familiar metaphor of this nation as being a "melting pot" has led to confusion and disagreement among researchers. Some believe that international students should become acculturated in that they should assimilate themselves into the American educational system, believe and behave like American students, and shake off characteristics of their cultural and ethnic backgrounds (Winkelman, 1994). Others believe that such acculturation is never fully possible; that cultural diversity is in itself a mark of the "American" culture; and that such diversity, in all of its manifestations, should be not only recognized but also honored, celebrated, and encouraged (Lonner & Ibrahim, 1996).

Rationale for the Book

The purpose of the book is to take a critical look at the adjustment problems as experienced by a group of international students at public universities in America and to provide them with information that will help with a smooth transition into the American academic community. Specifically, this study seeks to identify the adjustment problems of African students. Mori (2000) said international students on American college campuses are a diverse and increasing population whose unique concerns are traditionally overlooked. According to Thomas and Althen (1989), international students share certain characteristics regardless of their diverse cultural, social, religious, and political backgrounds. For instance, unlike other ethnic minorities, refugees, or recent immigrants, most international students plan to return to their home countries eventually and are in the US only temporarily. They are people in transition who choose to live in a foreign academic setting to realize their educational objectives. Because they are living far away from their families, relatives, and friends, they are also likely to have basic social support networks that are very distinct from those of American students. Faced with a new set of basic values and beliefs, international students are continually challenged to accommodate themselves to a variety of acculturation and adjustment problems. Moreover, international students have to deal with the same academic concerns faced by US students.

Despite the fact that international students, as a group, have many important commonalties, manifestations of their acculturative stress, culture adjustment issues, and help-seeking behavior vary depending on factors such as host culture/country ethnicity, gender, age, religious and linguistic backgrounds, sexual orientation, marital status, and area of residence in the US. Studies focusing on these factors are scarce. Arubayi (1981) suggested that international student adjustment could be better understood when studied in the context of the academic and social climate of the institution in which the international students are enrolled. Although colleges and universities often view foreign students as a source of diversity, enlightenment, and revenue, they must realize that these students also bring with them special needs. It is the responsibility of the institution to address these special needs, starting when these students arrive on campus. Therefore, this book contains valuable and rich information that will be available to African students and international student services departments, which hopefully will result in the development of better international student services and effective international orientation programs.

Definition of Terms

Adjustment: the process through which individuals become integrated into a new environment. It includes the satisfaction of one's motivations and needs.

Acculturation: the process of adapting the culture, or traits, or social patterns of another group (Winkelman, 1994).

Problems: any personal worries, concerns, fears, trouble, difficulty, or frustrations encountered by African students while studying in a college or university in the US. They may result in anxiety (worrisome feelings) and grief (deep sadness) (Meyer, 1984).

African Students: include individuals who are citizens of Africa and who are enrolled as students at any American college or university. These students are further identified as those who hold F-1 or J-1 non-immigrant status.

Foreign or International Students: refer to all students who are not citizens of the US and who are enrolled with a non-immigrant visa status studying in American colleges and universities. The terms "Foreign Students" and "International Students" are used synonymously.

Chapter II. Theories of Acculturation and

Adjustment

Introduction

The increase in pluralism and culture diversity in the US has been markedly reflected in its educational systems (Bradley, Parr, Lan, Bingi, & Gould, 1995). The size of the international student population in American universities has been steadily growing since the end of World War II (Das, Chow, & Rutherford, 1986; Sandhu, 1995). As an important center for information and advanced technology, the US has been consistently attracting many students and scholars worldwide (Sandhu, 1995). International students are located in more than 3,000 American institutions of higher education and represent over 186 nationalities (Institute of International Education, 2002).

International students on the American college campus are a diverse, increasing population whose unique acculturation concerns are traditionally overlooked (Mori, 2000). Given the current educational trend towards globalization, many institutions of higher learning are internationalizing their structure and curricula (Greene, 1998). In light of this internationalization process, educators often discuss the enrichment potential, beyond the financial benefits, that international students bring to the university atmosphere (Sandhu, 1995). However, research (Mori, 2000) suggests that the demands for acculturation/adjustment frequently place international students at greater risks for various problems than their American counterparts. In general, it is important that studies be done to help identify these problems.

Research has yielded somewhat limited support for the U-curve hypothesis, which postulates that at the start of the sojourn, the international student is likely to be excited by finally arriving in the US (and experiencing all the stimulation from the new environment) and generally feels optimistic and positive toward the host (Lysgaard, 1955). Other patterns of adjustment have also been identified (Verghese, 2002). For example, unlike the Scandinavian students in the earliest studies, some non-European students from Asia and

Africa followed an upside-down U-curve adjustment pattern (Verghese, 2002). Finally, a W-shaped curve has been identified when the process of readjustment to their home country post-sojourn was also included. Americanization can have different effects on these students as they re-enter a home culture, which may exhibit different levels of tolerance, or intolerance, for the students' newly found identity and attitudes (Winkelman, 1994).

Consideration of Adjustment Problems

Three factors emerge when considering the adjustment problems of international students. First, Klein et al (1971) suggested that in order to adequately predict or evaluate the behavior of international students, we must consider their specific culture. Therefore, it may not be fair to analyze and compare the experiences of a Venezuelan student with a Taiwanese student without considering the different cultural backgrounds of each. Behavior coming from an international student that appears to be inappropriate in the American culture may be acceptable if seen in the light of that student's own culture (Greene, 1998).

Secondly, attention must be given to the specific academic and social environments of the institution being studied (Kahne, 1976). For example, one study (Selby & Woods, 1962, as cited in Kahne, 1976) found that international student morale was higher during vacations and at the beginning of semesters and was lower at the end of the semesters and during examination time. They found that these trends could not be understood in terms of acculturation or culture shock.

The third factor was postulated by Maundeni (1999). Some of the problems and concerns that affect international students' adjustment to universities abroad are: personal, psychological, and academic problems; difficulties experienced in replacing a social network of family; concerns about political instabilities in their home country; finances; cultural differences; and food and climate issues. A number of researchers, including Adelegan and Parks (1985), Maundeni (1999), and Pruitt (1978), have also found that African students have trouble adjusting to life at universities abroad. However, little attention has been paid to identifying these problems.

Problems African Students Encounter Overseas (in America)

Prognosticators should not minimize the potential impact of the thousands of African students currently studying in this country. Among this group of students will be the political leaders, technicians, teachers, and the intellectual strength of many new countries in Africa that have emerged recently from colonial rule. The knowledge these students take with them when they leave American universities, and perhaps even more importantly the knowledge and experience gained from living in the US, can have major implications in their future. The information that these students take back to their countries will contribute to economic, social, and political growth.

In addition, American universities bear the responsibility of ensuring that whatever the African students do take back with them will enhance world cooperation, thereby providing educated individuals to their home countries. Although this study will be focusing on African students, it may apply to any international student. The study will have special significance for African students since they will be the social leaders of their developing countries tomorrow. One of the ways we can look at the effect of American schooling on these students is to assess any changes in their behaviors and attitudes occurring during the course of their education in American universities. An understanding of the adjustment problems that African students face while in America may be gained by university personnel.

Change of Environment

Many African students come from small towns and remote villages. Some of these areas do not have basic amenities such as electricity and piped water. When these students are suddenly taken from their homes and transferred overnight to a highly advanced and often intimidating large city, it is natural that they will face some serious adjustment problems. Some may manage to make the adjustment, albeit with great difficulty. Others adjust with little or no problems. Moreover, some may completely adapt to the different culture and customs in their desperate and immature attempt of the saying "when in Rome, do as the Romans do." Very often, these students return to Africa with different values. Therefore, it becomes extremely difficult to determine the level of impact their new values will have on the society. Livingstone (1960) observed that if the students respond too eagerly to their new environment, a possible conflict may ensue between the claims of two different worlds for these students. This situation has been described as the dilemma of overlapping membership. If the students seek to safeguard their cultural identity, their minds may harden against the many benefits the new experience brings. Either way, the students are assailed with doubts and anxieties that reduce working efficiency and produce mood swings of bewildering intensity. Somewhere along the way, most students come to terms with the unique demands made of them. Often, the result is at a greater cost than they had hoped to fulfill.

Difficulties with Living Abroad

College life is stressful and anxiety-producing for international students. This is due to a variety of factors, such as academics, social competition, and separation from family support (Huang, 1977). Because African students go overseas for further education, it is generally expected that they will encounter more difficulties adjusting than their African counterparts who have not gone abroad to study. These difficulties include communication problems, culture shock, adaptation to a new environment, conflicting social and moral values, and establishing social and professional relationships. Feelings of alienation, acquiring new housing and accommodations, and adjusting to a new educational system are all examples of the myriad of problems faced by international students studying outside their own countries (Altcher, 1976; Cable, 1974; Huang, 1977). Connoly (1967) stated that no matter how sincere and intelligent the students and no matter how prepared the college may be, the problems encountered are many. Adjustment to a new culture, which often includes an unmastered language, is extremely difficult. In addition, housing may be a problem because of the challenge of finding a place to live. The feeling of alienation caused by loneliness, the lack of social contact, and the prevalent conflict between reality and expectations is of traumatic proportions. Often, the result is complete disillusionment with the US, the university, and themselves. The students may return to their country with ambivalent or even hostile feelings about their visit and studies. Even more disconcerting is the fact that these students may return to their countries "Americanized" and unable or unwilling to adjust to their old environments.

This chapter has been organized in the following sequence: (a) Theories of Acculturation and Adjustment, (b) Patterns of Adjustment, and (c) Factors Affecting Adjustment.

Theories of Acculturation and Adjustment

As stated previously in Chapter I, The theory of acculturation focuses on understanding the adaptation processes and cultural changes of minority groups as they experience first-hand contact with a dominant culture (Sodowsky et al, 1991; Sodowsky & Plake, 1992). Originally, *acculturation* was defined as a process of cultural change that occurred at a group level (Redfield et al, 1936). Today, it is also recognized as a process occurring at an individual level, resulting in attitudinal and behavioral changes in an individual whose cultural group is mutually experiencing acculturation (Berry et al, 1987; Graves, 1967; Moyerman & Forman, 1992).

Although there are many models of acculturation, one of the most well-known models is the Bidirectional Acculturation Model (Berry, 1980, 1983). This model proposes that a minority person's psychological adjustment to a new culture can occur in four different ways: (1) integration, (2) assimilation, (3) rejection, and (4) deculturation. *Integration* refers to a person's desire to belong to the majority culture, whereas *assimilation* refers to the extent to which a person feels he or she has acculturated into the majority culture at the expense of his or her own culture. *Rejection* is defined as the tendency to reject the majority culture to maintain one's native culture. Finally, *deculturation* reflects the extent to which a person feels that he or she cannot identify with either the native or the majority culture. Differences that distinguish one culture from others are what provide individuals of the first culture with a unique sense of cultural identity. These differences are impossible to replicate in a foreign country. Therefore, the loss of cultural objects such as the symbolism of the national flag, music, and art, as well as numerous other background aspects of the home culture, can have a significant impact on the international student's quality of adjustment in the new environment.

Patterns of Adjustment

As a visitor, student, or traveler, whenever you go to a new place, whether it is a new country, school, or a new place of employment, you will face both the challenges of new cultural surroundings and the feelings of loss of a familiar cultural environment (Winkelman, 1994). Dealing with change is stressful. Facing the unknown can be anxiety-producing and fear-provoking. As a result, a person can experience the stimulation of learning new things, feelings of loss of familiar cultural cues and confusion, or cultural shock and adaptation (Winkelman, 1994). The following sections outline four generally agreed upon phases in acculturation adjustment (Winkelman, 1994).

Phase I: Honeymoon

Phase I is described as the honeymoon or tourist phase, typically experienced by honeymooners, vacationers, or those on brief business trips. For students, however, it is the application anxiety phase and is characterized by interest, excitement, sleeplessness, positive expectations, and idealizations about the new culture. Although anxiety and stress may be present, these tend to be interpreted positively.

Phase II: Crisis

Phase II is the crisis phase. The crisis phase may emerge immediately on arrival, or it may be delayed for some time, but it generally emerges within a few weeks to a month of arrival. It may start with a full-blown crisis or as a series of escalating problems, negative experiences, and reactions. Initial culture shock may start immediately for some individuals when they enter the airport or city. For others, it may develop over time. Although individual reaction varies, there are typical features: things start to go wrong, minor issues become major problems, and cultural differences become irritating. Excessive preoccupation with cleanliness of food, drinking water, bedding, and surroundings begins. One experiences increasing disappointments, frustrations, impatience, and tension. Life does not make sense, and some individuals may feel helpless, confused, disliked by others, or treated like a child. A sense of lack of control of one's life may lead to depression, isolation, anger, or hostility. Excessive emotionality and fatigue may be accompanied by physical or psychosomatic illness. One finds innumerable reasons to dislike and to criticize the (foreign) culture. Homesickness is common in this phase; one generally wants to go home. For students, this arrival/initial culture shock stage is shown in the adjustment cycle diagram (*Figure 2.1*).

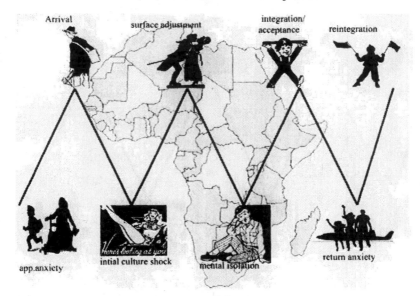

Figure 2.1. Adjustment/Acculturation Phases.

Phase III: Adjustment and Orientation

        Phase III involves adjustment and orientation (surface adjustment phase). This phase is concerned with learning how to adjust effectively to the new cultural environment. A stated previously in Chapter I, resolution of cultural shock lies in learning how to make an acceptable adaptation to the new culture. A variety of adjustments will be achieved during cyclical and individually unique adjustment phases. There may be an adjustment without adaptation, such as flight or isolation. Many people who move to foreign countries do not effectively adapt; instead, they opt to return home during the crisis phase. Others use various forms of isolation; for example, living in an ethnic enclave and avoiding substantial learning about the new culture, which is mental isolation. If one desires to function effectively, it is necessary to adjust and adapt. One develops problem-solving skills for dealing with the culture and begins to accept the cultural differences with a positive attitude. The culture begins to make sense, and negative reactions and responses to the culture are reduced as one recognizes that problems are due to the inability to understand, accept, and adapt. An appreciation of the other culture begins to emerge, and learning about it becomes a fun challenge. During the adjustment phase, the problems do not end, but one develops a positive attitude toward meeting the challenge of resolving the issues necessary to function in the new culture. Adjustment is slow, involving recurrent crises and readjustments.

Phase IV: Adaptation

        Phase IV, the final phase, involves adaptation, resolution, acceptance, or acculturation. This phase is achieved as one develops stable adaptations and becomes successful at resolving problems and managing the new culture. There are many different adaptation options, especially given diverse individual characteristics and goals. Although full assimilation is difficult, if not impossible, one may undergo substantial personal changes through cultural adaptation and the development of a bicultural identity. It is important to recognize and accept the fact that an effective adaptation will not necessarily change the individual, leading to the development of a bicultural identity and the integration of new cultural aspects into one's previous self-concept. Reaching this stage requires a constructive response to cultural shock with effective means of adaptation.

Repetition of Phases

These four phases are both sequential and cyclical. The shift from crisis to adjustment and adaptation can repeat as one encounters new crises, requiring additional adjustments. Winkelman (1994) concluded that students or travelers may become effectively bicultural as the adaptation phase becomes permanent.

Factors Affecting Adjustment

Eddy (1978) stated that the international student experience actually begins before arrival at a college or university in the US. In essence, the student must make a choice concerning the type and place of education. To make this choice requires the kind of background knowledge that even American students find difficult to obtain. Eddy further stated that after entering the US, students face the following barriers: language, academic advice, economic problems, cultural assimilation, reentry problems, and age.

Language

Eddy (1978) stated that the first barrier for international students to encounter is language. The majority of international students come from countries where English is not the first language. Sasnett (1950) believed that these students' academic success rests to a large degree on their ability to understand and speak English. Almost all the research concerning international students refers to English as being one of the most difficult problems encountered. Georgiades (1981) indicated that international students who choose English as their preferred means of communication reported no problems, as evidenced in the findings of the 11 problem areas of the Michigan International Student Problem Inventory (MISPI). Students who chose their native language as their preferred means of communication on the same instrument reported a possible problem using the English language.

Academic Advice

Eddy (1978) believed that the American educational system might also become an obstacle to international students' education. Degree requirements, course structure, course content, and academic standards may be quite different in American universities as compared to similar institutions in the international students' home countries. Students studying in America may be confused by their course options and program organization.

Economic Problems

Economic problems are of great concern to international students (Eddy, 1978). Those who come to the US with limited resources may experience financial difficulties. These difficulties are a result of one or a combination of the following reasons: students estimated their expenses with inadequate information provided in the college catalog, students had unrealistic ideas about the availability of financial aid or other sources of income, students did not anticipate inflation, students changed or extended their coursework, or students over spent their monies buying American consumer goods.

Cultural Assimilation

Sunberg (1977) stated that all human beings, regardless of cultural origin, share many similarities such as physical similarities and the developmental stages of birth, childhood, adulthood, and old age. However, individual students identify with their own group and not all of humankind. To international students, understanding American behavior and adjusting to it may be a difficult task. Upon their arrival in the US, their normal daily activities are interrupted, vastly changed, or sometimes abandoned. Hendricks and Skinner (1975) noted that many factors come into play in the cultural assimilation of international students. First, the students' legal status as an alien may imply to the domestic students that the international students are transients in the American society. They are then branded from the onset as outsiders. As a foreigner, the students may not have a clear idea of what is expected of them, how much Americans assume they understand, or how many questions they should ask. Cultural differences in friendship building, dating etiquette, or even aggressiveness may be confusing to international students. Further, the weather or climate may add to the difficulties of adjustment.

Studies of social adjustment indicate that international students are frequently isolated from social activities (Coan, 1971; Klein et al., 1971), having little interaction with American students (Deutsch, 1965). Of the 447 international students surveyed at the University of Tennessee, Alsaffar (1977) found that most of these students spent their available time with friends of their own co-national groups. Those groups indicated limited involvement with the various activities on or off campus. Overall, it appears that international students prefer more involvement with their own co-national groups (Coan, 1971; Spaulding & Flack, 1976). This preference is evidenced by the tendency to create small "communities" within the host country. International students who congregate together and communicate with one another experience fewer coping problems than those who fail to establish identity with a co-national group.

With respect to participation of the international students in various activities on and off campus, Reiff (cited in Perkins, Perkins, Guglielmino, and Reiff, 1977) reported that almost half of the international students at the University of Georgia belonged to an association of their particular nationality. He stated that the more students there were of a particular nationality and the more differences there were between their countries and the US, the more likely the group was to form an association.

With respect to living arrangements, Coan (1971) reported that not many international students live in university residence halls because many, especially those coming from Asian and African countries, find it difficult to adjust to American food. Hence, international students live mostly in groups comprised of members of their own country and do their own cooking. Thus, there is a strong tendency to inbreed among these students. They live as a group, socializing mostly among themselves, and develop certain commonly biased notions about the larger American society.

Reentry Problems

Eddy (1978) noted that for those students who do return to their home countries after completion of their studies, the reentry process is very complex. After four or more years away from home, reentry may be very much like the entry experience with the US, in the sense that it requires reacculturation. Reentry is the transition process during which foreign students return to their home countries. The process begins with anticipation of and preparation for return and continues through reacculturation at home. Cultural, social, religious, economic, linguistic, political, educational, and professional adjustments may be necessary. Some students will be eager to return home, others may have mixed feelings, and still others may have come to feel considerable alienation from their own cultures. Marsh (1975) discussed the "role shock" that foreign students may experience when they are not automatically seen as change agents on return to their home countries. The students probably come to consider themselves well educated and sophisticated and may find that their countrymen do not perceive them in the same way. Karla (1974) pointed out that there is serious underemployment for many of these scholars, especially in developing countries where government support does not match the scholars' talents. It is likely, too, that many graduates will be unable to continue their professional development, either at home or by making occasional visits to the US. In the end, this situation tends to work against both the individuals and one of the major objectives of international educational exchange, which is to set in motion and perpetuate the development of nations by the education of their native inhabitants with particular reference to Africa, due to the continent's lack of economic and political stability and technological advancement.

Age

Another factor, mentioned by DuBois (1965), is age. DuBois believed that the age of a student is an important factor in sojourn adjustment. Younger students tend to stay in the US longer, but educators and international student advisors favor older (graduate) students over younger (undergraduate) students. Graduates are preferred because of their maturity, the possibility of a shorter stay, less potential of causing problems, and having definite goals. Furthermore, graduate students are considered less subject to alienation and need less counseling.

Summary

This chapter presented a review of literature related to the adjustment problems encountered by international students, including African students, while studying in American colleges and universities.

In response to the increasing number of international students, there has been an increasing amount of literature published that has addressed the specific needs, unique experiences, and adjustment problems of these students (Essandoh, 1995; Hayes & Lin, 1994; Pedersen, 1991; Sandhu, 1995). Several studies have reported that many international students have difficulty adjusting to the American culture and academic expectations (Pedersen, 1991; Sandhu & Asrabadi, 1994). Furthermore, students from developing nations have been found to have a higher level of difficulty in their adjustment process (Pedersen, 1991).

International students are subjected to the same stresses of academic and personal life as their American counterparts. These stresses, however, are compounded by their being plunged into an unfamiliar culture and surrounded by a language of which the students have limited understanding. Acculturation theory provides researchers with a mechanism for studying the adjustment of international students in the US (Winkelman, 1994).

Previous research in this area was conducted about two decades ago. Other studies deal with quantifiable facts, such as are often found in a questionnaire or survey. Although we are still dealing with subjective data, individual perceptions of what is considered problematic, using objective, factual forms of data collection, make statistical or technical analysis more possible. As we approach the process of analyzing international student adjustment, particularly African students, this book has the potential of leading to a balanced perspective of adjustment problems of African students in public universities. Furthermore, studies underline the difficulties that many African students have during their stay as students in America (Gabriel, 1973; and Arubayi, 1980). Before arrival into the US, many of these students expect a smooth transition and easiness of making American friends, but few of them do. Therefore, it has been proven over and over again that orientation programs are the life line that all international students need for a truly smooth transition.

Chapter III. International Orientation

Program

Introduction

All international student orientation and registration programs are organized by the Office of International Student Services (OISS) at all universities in America. A typical example is that of Western Michigan University (WMU). The OISS was established in 1968 under the Student Services Division of the University. The purpose of the Office is to:

- Admit all foreign students;

- Evaluate foreign credentials, English-speaking ability, and finances;

- Recruit new students to the institution;

- Offer an international student orientation and registration program;

- Counsel and/or advise foreign students on personal and economic concerns, institutional procedures, and problems;

- Serve as liaison between the office and various campus-based foreign student organizations;

- Serve as consultants to faculty, staff, and other people both inside and outside the university regarding the academic, financial, and/or social status of foreign students;

- Act as an information resource center for international students;

- Maintain student records and files of international students;

- Help international students find employment in their home countries after completion of their studies; and

- Prepare and disseminate resource material guidelines, handbooks, or similar materials to foreign students.

At the University of Indiana at Bloomington the OISS mission is to foster cross-cultural understanding and enable international students and scholars to accomplish their educational, social, and professional objectives. Most universities achieve these goals through a wide range of quality services, including immigration and financial advising, ongoing orientation, and cultural programs. Therefore, the international orientation program is more than just the first two, three, or four days on campus for international students. The program is the first two, three, or four days of their entire college career.

Admission to a University

A familiar letter that all of us receive after our admission process is completed is of the congratulatory nature. The letter generally begins "Congratulations on your admission to our university. We look forward to welcoming you to your university and introducing you to your new community. The Office of International Students is pleased that you have chosen our university for furthering your studies in America. The university community is committed to furthering international understanding, and you will be a valuable asset to this process."

The next phase of your educational sojourn to your university, now that you have been accepted, is starting to plan your trip. You will need to:

- Obtain your passport and American visa as soon as possible because the process does take time;

- Make travel arrangements to your university by buying your airline tickets;

- Make arrangements for money to be sent in advance or you can bring it with you, but for security reasons, it is better to send it in advance;

- Arrange for a place to stay during the orientation program because in most cases, during the orientation period, most schools are not formally in session;

- Be sure you advise your friends and family of your temporary mailing address; and

- Be sure you visit the institution's web site to learn more about the university and international student organizations that are offered and how they can assist you.

Preparing for Arrival

After getting your visa and booking your flight to your university, and as your arrival time draws nearer, make sure you have obtained the following information:

- Confirmation that your tuition fees have been received by the Office of the Bursar;

- Correct information about on-campus housing availability, acquired by visiting the web site of residential programs and services, especially if you have a question about the status of your housing application or contact (applications can be downloaded from the web site); off-campus housing information can also be obtained about apartment houses and townhouses of various sizes, along with the advantages of saving money by sharing the cost of housing, utilities (electric/power, telephone, and in some cases gas and water), and food (by having a kitchen to cook your own meals) with your roommates;

- Correct information about methods of transportation from the airport to the school upon arrival; some schools do make special arrangements to pick people up from the airport; and

- Information about when and where the orientation program will take place; some schools charge for the orientation program, and it is usually added to your financial account.

Importance of the International Orientation Program

University of Wisconsin at Madison

According to Pamela Oliver of the University of Wisconsin at Madison (2002), with the new climate in the US after September 11 and the investigations going on across the country, we want to take all precautions and not place our international students at risk by allowing them to fail compliance with the Immigration and Naturalization Service (INS) regulations. Therefore, the importance of orientation programs for international students nationwide cannot be over emphasized.

Western Michigan University (WMU)

According to WMU, the mission statement and goals of their International Orientation Program are as follows. "The mission of the Western Michigan University International Orientation Program is to provide a comprehensive experience, which will aid new students in their transition to the institution, expose new students to the educational opportunities within Western Michigan University, integrate new students into the academic and campus life of the institution, increase the retention rate of new international students, assist them to understand the university environment and services, and enhance new awareness of issues facing new college students in American universities." Having the focus on new international students, the main goals of the WMU International Orientation Program are to:

- Help students with housing;
- Advise students of degree requirements needed for graduation and assist with appropriate program selection prior to registration;
- Provide instructions for the telephone registration procedures;
- Inform students of language restrictions placed on their enrollment;
- Inform students of organizations, cultural, and social activities on campus;

- Assist students in locating their major's advising office, the Administration Building, Sinddecuse Health Center, Bernhard Center, Waldo Library, and Ellsworth Hall;

- Present students with materials and information explaining grading and academic study requirements at WMU prior to registration for classes;

- Arrange for the students to know others more significantly by the end of the program than at the beginning;

- Ensure that students are aware of the basic immigration requirements;

- Require students to visit their major department offices and identify locations of their major academic advisor's office prior to registration for classes; and

- Assist students in opening bank accounts and obtaining Bronco cards (identity cards) and Michigan ID.

Yale University

According to the Office of International Students and Scholars (OISS) of Yale University, "International Orientation will serve as an introduction to the University community, giving you a capsulated view of the variety of opportunities available to you. During orientation, you complete all necessary procedures for class registration, including placement testing, general information sessions, and academic advising. Orientation also gives you a chance to meet other new students and talk to current international and American students." Here is what participants had to say about past orientation programs:

"Orientation is a great way to meet new students and get yourself acclimated to the Northern State University community."

"It was great to meet both the new students and the other upperclassmen leaders at the same time. It was such a diverse group of leaders."

"The program served its purpose perfectly. It was not only a great first step for me into the US, but most important of all, it was a great first step into the Yale community. In the OISS, I have found much more than I expected. I highly recommend it to every international newcomer."

"The most important task for the OISS is to have the international students get to know each other, and that they did indeed."

"Just meeting students who were in the same situation relieved me and also stimulated me at the same time. It was a great way to get Yale experience before hand."

"OISS didn't meet my expectations – it surpassed them! I absolutely loved the entire program. It was fun, enlightening, entertaining, and completely satisfying. I was truly inspired – it ROCKED! It provided me with the perfect welcome to Yale."

Overall Program Significance

Therefore, in a nutshell, the International Orientation Program is designed specifically to assist newly admitted international students in adjusting to their various campuses. For these reasons, make it a very high priority to attend the orientation program. Attendance is mandatory because it is your license to a smooth transition into your university.

Summary

With the new climate in the US after September 11, the situation has changed for all international students coming to America for study. As such, the international orientation program has become so important that all new international students must attend. The main objective of the orientation program at various universities cannot be stated more wisely than the mission statement provided by WMU (see Importance of the International Orientation Program). If at the end of the orientation program participants explicitly make comments such as "The program served its purpose perfectly. It was not only a great first step for me into the US, but most important of all, it was a great first step into the Yale community. In the OISS, I have found much more than I expected. I highly recommend it to every international newcomer," it proves how valuable and important the orientation program is to new international students.

Therefore, you are most welcome to your university, and I hope that your stay will be pleasant, memorable, and successful. You must remember that the primary objective of your coming to America is education. The least but not the last important consideration is that moving from one culture, time zone, and physical environment into another presents certain difficulties, such as physical, mental, and social challenges. Therefore, the next chapter will provide you with basic but important information on how to survive in America.

Chapter IV. How to Survive in America

Introduction

I would like to welcome you to the US. As international students leave their home environment, they lose a familiar support system, especially in Africa, where people generally are dependent on each other. Pedersen (1991) suggested that loss of a support system can result in increased anxiety and loss of self-esteem. Research has shown that many international students experience a lack of resources and support to deal with situations, such as culture, social, academic, economic, etc. (Heikinheimo & Shute, 1986; Pedersen, 1991). Therefore, this chapter will provide you with life-saving information that will help your stay at your university be more pleasant, memorable, and successful.

Although personality differences influence the severity of the adjustment process, all international students will experience them to a greater or lesser degree, whatever their country of origin, sex, area of study, or age. However, research over a period of 20 years seems to support the hypothesis that age is a greater barrier to adjustment, that women suffer more adjustment problems, and that those who come from very different cultural and academic environments like Africa are more likely to have greater difficulty adapting to the American culture. Nevertheless, the adjustment process can impact individuals very differently; it is considered to be a difficult, reactive, and conflicting process rather than a smooth transition. The process is considered difficult and reactive because, especially for African students, many may be financially liable to their home government, foreign governments, or to their families. To fail or to perform poorly could result in shame not only to the individual involved, but also to the family. As Africans, we cannot afford to fail because our families would be disappointed, and we do not want that to happen. If I fail, it is not only that I fail. It also means that my father's son and my uncle's nephew failed, and both failures carry the same reputation (Heikinheimo, 1986).

Public Safety (Police Department)

Every public university has a police department on campus. They are the law enforcement agency for the university. All campus police officers are certified by the state and have the same authority as any city, county, or state agency officers. The campus police department is responsible for the protection of both life and property on these campuses as well as enforcement of local and state laws.

The mission of the campus police department is to provide a crime-free environment through the efforts of a team of professional law enforcement officers working together with the campus community. Accomplishing this goal and ensuring a safe and healthy environment creates an ideal atmosphere for the promotion of learning and fosters high standards of research. The police department, in most cases, consists of three departments, namely (1) Crime Prevention and Training, (2) Patrol and Investigations, and (3) Security and Detective.

Crime Prevention and Training Division

The *Crime Prevention and Training Division* is responsible not only for training the police officers, but also for maintaining their training records, thereby ensuring they all meet state law enforcement minimum standards. In addition, the division gives crime prevention handouts and presentations on- and off-campus during new employee orientation, student orientation, etc.

Patrol and Investigations Divisions

The *Patrol Division* is responsible for maintaining a safe environment on the campus through enforcement of state statutes, local ordinances, and regulations upheld by the various universities by conducting pro-active, preventative patrol to include vehicle, foot, scooter, and bicycle patrol to assure the safety of the university community. The *Investigations Division* conducts preliminary and latent investigations of all incidents, which require police assistance.

Security and Detective Divisions

The *Security Division* is responsible for setting up, monitoring, and maintaining the campus-wide security system. Part of the Security division's responsibilities will be installing and maintaining surveillance equipment. The *Detective Division* mainly operates the Lost and Found. If you lost anything while on campus or in any of its parking areas, contact them by email or by calling the police department's number.

Whenever you need assistance, make sure you call the on-campus emergency assistance number. For off-campus emergencies, call 911. The following are crime prevention tips that are very important:

- Remember the location of all blue-light emergency phones that are located throughout the campus for your safety;

- Be alert for suspicious people loitering on campus and notify a friend or the campus police immediately;

- You are encouraged to secure your personal property and valuables at all times;

- If you are studying late and have reason to be apprehensive about getting to your vehicle, dormitory, or apartment, call the campus police for an escort;

- Contact the police if you see anything that looks like a potential threat to the safety and security of anyone or anything in or around the campus;

- Never give your bankcard PIN to anyone claiming to be a bank employee or even the police; and

- Please observe all posted speed limits and traffic laws.

Remember, we can all make a difference, and with your help, we can make your campus a safe learning environment.

Housing

It is important to remember that moving from one culture creates initial feelings of uneasiness, which certainly creates physical, mental, and social challenges. Therefore, the number one challenge is finding a place to live. Students in America have many housing options.

Dormitories (Residence Halls)

Dormitories are usually located on or very near the campus, making them accessible to classes. Food and sometimes cleaning services are provided. Dormitories are usually crowded and noisy, making it difficult for one to study and find privacy. However, living in this environment also gives you the opportunity to make new friends due to the large number of students living in dormitories.

Family Housing

Most universities provide *family housing* to certain students. This type of housing is available only to mature and married students. Sometimes, these individuals have children who live with them in the family housing units.

Fraternity/Sorority Houses (Student Organizations)

Some fraternities and sororities own large houses where many of their members stay together. You must be a member to live in these houses.

Apartments

Apartments are housing complexes that are comprised of one, two, or three bedrooms and one or two bathrooms, in addition to a kitchen and living room (parlor). Apartment management will usually enforce the number of people allowed to live together in each apartment. Apartments located near campus are more expensive than those that are farther away. Most of them have amenities, such as laundry machines (some are coin operated); parking; tennis courts; group meeting rooms; and a fitness center, playground for kids, and swimming pool. Garbage removal and lawn or yard work is the responsibility of the apartment management.

Studio (Efficiency) Apartments

Studio apartments provide a cheap alternative if you want to live alone. They are small, with living and sleeping areas all in one room. Some do provide cooking areas.

Single-Family Homes (Houses)

Single-family homes are much more expensive to rent, and as such, it is advisable that you share expenses with two, three or four students. In addition, the cost of all utilities (heat, electricity and/or gas, water, garbage removal, and telephone) and lawn or yard work is your responsibility.

Affordable Housing

The next big question is "How do I find *affordable housing?*" According to the International Students INC (ISI) handbook (1995) *How to Survive in the US*, for information on dormitories and family housing, contact the international student office or campus housing agency. For fraternity and sorority housing information, contact the fraternity or sorority in which you interested. You may want to find a roommate with whom you want to live in an apartment or house and to share expenses.

Rental Deposit

A *deposit* is a sum of money paid by individuals living in a rented apartment or house to guarantee against damage to the building. If there is no damage and you clean the apartment or house thoroughly before you move out, your landlord or apartment manager should return most or all of the deposit. Most states require the landlord to return the deposit money to you within 30 days after you move.

Lease Agreement

A *lease* is a written agreement, or contract, between the tenant(s) and landlord. A lease usually states the following:

- Monthly rental amount;
- Date rent is due every month (in America, you are expected to take the rent to your landlord or apartment leasing office on or before the day it is due or mail it early enough so it arrives by the day it is due; late payments do attract extra charges);
- Amount of deposit;
- Length of time you are required to stay (for example, 6 or 12 months);
- Which utilities you are expected to pay;
- Amount of notice (number of days) you must give before moving out;
- Rules you must follow (i.e., no pets);
- Services the landlord agrees to perform (i.e., yard work or repairs); and
- Other conditions the landlord and you agree to follow.

As they say it in America, make sure you read the fine lines of your lease because it is a legally binding contract; as such, read it very carefully and thoroughly before signing it.

Other Housing Issues

Check bulletin or notice boards, or check the schools or city newspapers under the sections "Roommates" or "Rooms for Rent" in the classified advertisements. Before you finally make up your mind about which type of housing best meets your needs, consider the following:

- Find out how much you need to pay for rent;

- Read an Apartment Shopper's Guide or other publications that provide information on rent costs (these guides can be found at the housing office, student centers, and convenience and grocery stores on campus);

- Make sure you use an apartment referral agency that will help you find housing without any fee; and

- Explore the Yellow Pages of your telephone book under "Apartment Finding and Rental Service."

Most importantly, before you move in with a friend, another student, or a family, the following issues must be discussed extensively, according to ISI:

- What portion of the rent and utilities will each person be expected to pay?

- What household chores will each person assume?

- Will you purchase food and cook together or separately?

- What hours are you allowed having guests, watching television, or playing your stereo above a reasonable volume?

- What rules regarding drinking alcohol and smoking will you have in the dwelling?

- Will you share a telephone or purchase separate telephones and services?

- How much advance notice should each individual give before moving out?

Acquiring Furniture

You might be wondering where you can get furniture. If you rent a furnished apartment, it has the following basics: bed, couch, table, and chairs. The rent might be a little higher, but for an unfurnished apartment, you may wish to check second-hand (used) or thrift (i.e., Goodwill, Salvation Army, etc.) stores, garage or yard sales, flea markets, bulletin boards on campus, and the newspaper classified advertisement section. In addition, you can ask members of your church or mosque for help with used furnishing.

Transportation

According to ISI, the public transportation systems in most cities in America are not as developed as in many countries. At the university in your city, you might find the following: subways, city-operated buses, shuttle buses, and taxis. In addition, you may wish to purchase a car at some point.

Subways

   Subways are underground trains that usually operate 24 hours per day, 7 days per week. They are found mostly in larger cities and often run between the suburbs (outlying areas) and the downtown area. Maps and schedules are available from the ticket office. Always make sure you ask an American friend to assist if you have to use the subway. You can save money by purchasing a multiple-ride ticket or monthly pass.

City-Operated Buses

   Buses are city-operated, which involves taking you to different places like the malls, hospitals, stadiums, etc. Maps and schedules are available at local banks, certain shops and libraries, and student centers and on the bus or from the bus driver. Remember, buses run primarily during the day. You can get on or off a bus at designated stops, which are usually located every few blocks along the route. Fare is paid by exact change in coins, multiple-ride tickets, or monthly passes. Ask if student discounts are available.

Shuttle Buses

   Shuttle buses are usually operated by the university or in conjunction with the city and run mostly around the campus. These are often free or cost a small amount.

Taxis

   Taxis are generally more expensive. Therefore, before you use a taxi, be sure you ask about the fee before you agree to ride. The driver usually expects a tip of 15% of the fare in addition to what you are supposed to pay. Be warned that unless it is absolutely necessary, you should not use a taxi.

Purchasing a Car

   When you are ready to buy a *car*, please make sure you seek advice from a fellow student who has been at your school for more than one year or an American friend who owns a car and is familiar with the car-buying process. You may buy a car from an individual dealer or a dealership (sells new and used cars), from the classified section under automobiles, or by driving around neighborhoods during the weekend. You may also check for postings on bulletin boards, etc.

Other Car-Related Issues and Insurance

   In America, if you choose to buy a car, remember that you will also have to pay for *license plates*, *insurance*, *repairs*, *gasoline*, and *parking*. Most states require car *insurance*, and failure to have insurance will result in a traffic ticket, fine, or even a court hearing. Contact an insurance agent about buying an insurance policy, which serves to protect you and is a contract that describes the amount of money the insurance company will pay for specific damages. You will pay premiums (a certain amount of money every month, every six months, or once a year) based on the policy coverage (types of damages for which the policy will pay and how much it will pay).

Most states require you to have premiums for *liability insurance*, which means the insurance company will pay for damage to another car if you are responsible for the accident. If you purchase *collision insurance*, which is strongly recommended, the insurance company will pay for damages to your car. *Comprehensive insurance* covers damage caused by things such as weather, vandalism, or theft. Most insurance policies require you to pay a deductible, a certain amount of money you pay prior to repairing damages, with the insurance agency paying for anything above that specified amount. For example, if you have a $250 deductible on your collision insurance and you have an accident that causes $1,000 in damages to your car, according to ISI, you would pay the first $250, and the insurance company would pay $750. The higher the deductible amount on the insurance policy, the lower your premiums will be.

Acquiring a Driver's License

For those who can drive, remember that before you drive, you must get a new *driver's license*. Check your local motor vehicle or revenue office, since driving rules vary from state to state. First and foremost, you will have to apply at one of these offices, where you will be required to take a written test on the laws for driving in that state (a booklet of state laws is available at the office or a branch of the Secretary of State's Office). You will also need to pass a vision test. Therefore, if you need glasses or contact lenses, make sure you wear them. In addition, you must pass an actual driving test. If you fail the written and/or driving test, you can take them again. For those who do not know how to drive, you can sign up for driving school lessons, whereby a trained professional will teach you how to drive a car for a fee. You can also solicit the help of friends who have their driving licenses.

Shopping

Types of Stores

Discount and Department Stores

As you go shopping, remember there are two types of stores from which you can choose. *Discount stores* (i.e., K-Mart, Wal-Mart, Target, and Big Lots) offer a good selection of items at lower prices and are mostly self-service. While *department stores* (i.e., Sears, JCPenney, Old Navy, Kohls, and TJ Maxx) generally have higher prices but better quality products as well as salespeople who are available to assist you.

Drug Stores (Pharmacy)

A *drug store* consists of a pharmacy where you can buy prescription (medicine that a doctor has advised you to take) and nonprescription drugs, such as cold and headache remedies, vitamins, and other common medicines for sickness. Nonprescription medications can be bought without a doctor's prescription. According to ISI, drug stores also sell generic medicines at a lower cost than brand-name drug products. To get generic medicines, you must specifically request a generic substitution when ordering you prescription. A drug store sells much more than drugs. In most drug stores, you can also buy cosmetics, household items, toys, stationery, and often even food and clothing.

Grocery Stores

A typical *grocery store* sells food. Grocery store chains, which may vary from region to region (i.e., Kroger, Miejer, Harvest Foods, etc.), have many stores that operate on a larger basis and offer a wide variety of foods, including most meats, fruits, frozen foods, boxed foods, vegetables, etc. They also sell non-food items such as soap, cleaning supplies, health care products, bathroom supplies, and so forth. There are also some discount-chain grocery stores, such as Save-A-Lot Foods, Cub Foods, and Food 4 Less, that offer a large variety of foods and other items at a lesser price, but you must stack and carry your own groceries at the checkout line.

Convenience Stores

Convenience stores, such as 7-Eleven and Quick Trip, sell food and other items (i.e., household products and things for your car). They are usually open 24 hours per day, 7 days per week, but their prices are higher, and they have a limited selection of items.

Local or Neighborhood Grocery Stores

Neighborhood grocery stores are much bigger and offer a greater variety of items (i.e., meats, fruits, and vegetables) than the convenience stores. They are often more convenient than the larger grocery chains, but you pay higher prices as well.

Garage, Yard, or Moving Sales

Garage sales (also referred to as yard or moving sales) contain mostly used, excess, or unneeded items (i.e., clothing, books, toys, furniture, computers, and other household items). Families and individuals hold these sales at their homes in their garages and yards. The sales are mostly done during the weekend and during spring/summer in the Midwest and East. However, sales in the South and West are held almost year-round because of the weather. Bargaining is accepted at these sales. In some cases, most prices are fixed and cannot be changed through bargaining, but when buying items that cost a lot of money (i.e., a washer and dryer set or living room and dining room furniture), bargaining can take place. A safe way out, if you are not sure whether to bargain, is simply to ask whether the price is "fixed" or "set".

Second-Hand (Thrift) Stores

Second-hand or *thrift stores*, such as Goodwill, Salvation Army, or Pawn Shops, are good places to look for used furniture, clothing, and household items (i.e., pots, dishes, television, computers, etc.). A word of caution: make sure you check all used items carefully for any damages before you purchase them.

International Foods

In bigger cities, there are small, medium, and large grocery stores that sell *international foods* for specific countries (i.e., Asian, African, and South American). Restaurants serving foods from your countries can also be found. Generally, a tip (a cash gratuity left on the table for the server) is expected by the waiter or waitress who serves you. The acceptable percentage is 15% of the total cost of the meal. Some restaurants will automatically add this 15% gratuity charge to your bill if you have a certain number of people (i.e., seven or more) in your dining party. In addition, some of restaurants would like you to make reservations while others do not.

Shopping Malls

According to ISI, a *shopping mall* consists of many stores housed together under one roof. Most malls have discount stores, departmental stores, specialty shops, restaurants, pet stores, and sometimes even movie theaters. This makes window shopping and comparing prices on similar items at different stores easier, giving one the advantage of making a good buy.

Modes of Payment

Cash versus Credit or Debit Cards

For all business transactions, sales clerks will ask clerks whether you want to pay by "cash or charge". In other words, the clerk wants to know whether you will be paying *cash* (actual money or personal check) or charging it to your credit or debit card. Credit and debit cards are similar to checks because you can buy items without having cash. *Credit cards* are very convenient because you can use them almost anywhere you travel in America, and you do not need to keep a record of a balance because you will receive a monthly bill for all credit card purchases. *Debit cards* can also be used almost anywhere you travel, but they must display either the Visa or MasterCard symbol. Although you have the option to keep track of your balance, you should make it a habit because transactions made using the debit card will affect your checking account. Nevertheless, you will receive a detailed description of all purchases on your monthly bank statement.

Major, Retail, and Gasoline Credit Cards

Several types of credit cards exist. *Major credit cards*, such as Visa, MasterCard, and American Express, allow you to buy almost any item from any type of business. *Retail credit cards* from large stores, such as JC Penny and Sears, allow you to purchase items only at those particular stores. *Gasoline credit cards* from oil companies, such as Shell, Conoco, and Exxon Mobile, allow you to buy gasoline, other items, and services only from their service stations (ISI).

Credit Card Applications

Not everyone who applies for a credit card gets one. Initially, you must fill out an *application* showing how much income you receive and how may bills you have. Most credit card companies now run a credit check (background of your credit obligations) on individuals. If the credit card company decides that you do not make enough money or have too many bills to pay, they will not approve you for a credit card (ISI). I would like to offer you a word of caution and advice. Unless it is absolutely necessary, do not obtain or apply for a credit card. Ask an officer in the International student services for more details about any credit card before applying for one.

Annual Fees

Most credit card companies charge an *annual fee* to use their credit cards. Remember also that these companies are charging you a high annual interest rate on your charge balance. Therefore, be sure you pay the entire balance for all purchases when the amount is due because if you do not pay the full balance, you are going to be charged interest on the remaining amount and possibly a late fee charge (if the payment is not made timely).

Sales Taxes

On every receipt you get from purchases made in stores, you will see an amount for *sales tax*. Sales tax is an extra charge (mandated by local and state governments) that is added onto the price of an item at the time of the purchase. For gasoline, the sales tax is already added into the purchase price. The percentage for the sales tax and the items subject to the tax vary from state to state.

Typical American Classroom Situation

Each university is run differently. If you have questions concerning issues, such as registration, schedules, tuition, and testing methods, consult your foreign student adviser, other students, your departmental academic adviser, or a an American friend. Remember, it is important that you start on a solid foundation. At the first class meeting, most professors will hand out a course syllabus listing the objectives of the class and other important information, such as grades, assignments, quizzes, and midterm and final examinations. Furthermore, these course guides generally mention required textbooks, term papers (i.e., research papers), test dates, dates that projects must be completed, and criteria for grading your performance. Very rarely will your grade be based on just the final examination. Most professors use slightly different grading systems, and they will explain the grading system the first day of class. Most teachers prefer or require you to type papers or reports in a specific manner. If you cannot type, you may want to consider paying someone to type your papers.

Classroom Etiquette, Grades, and studying

Professors in American classrooms primarily lecture to students. Students do not rise in acknowledgment when the professor enters the lecture hall or classroom. They interrupt their teachers with questions, forcefully argue points with which they disagree, sometimes eat food during class, or get up to leave whenever they choose. In most classrooms, teachers encourage discussion. If you have a question or even wish to challenge something the teacher has said, you should not be afraid to raise your hand and speak up when called on. Sometimes teachers will base your grade partly on your participation in class discussions because it indicates to the teacher that you have read and understand the material you are studying. If you feel uncomfortable with the language or the classroom method, make sure you schedule an appointment to see the teacher to explain your difficulty to him or her. Depending on your course load and your major, you may have to study more than what you have been used to in the past. Seek the help of other older international students on campus about studying habits. Some universities do offer special tutoring classes and assistance for writing papers and completing assignments, especially for those of us with English as our second language. You should take advantage of all of these opportunities.

Acceptable Behavior

A difference in what is proper, acceptable, and expected student behavior varies between universities, among departments within each university, and with each individual teacher. A good way to learn what is acceptable behavior is to observe other students (ISI).

Types and Consequences of Cheating

The following instances are considered cheating: having someone else to complete an assignment for you, copying someone else's work and submitting it as your own, and looking at another student's work during a test. The teacher has the authority to remove some or all of the points from the student's test or paper, or the student may fail the entire class if caught cheating. Many universities require students who are caught cheating to appear before an honor board (similar to a court) to determine the punishment, which in some cases may include expulsion. Each university has specific policies governing investigation and punishment of cheating.

Giving Gifts

In America, according to ISI, it is not customary to give gifts to teachers, nor will the gifts have any effect on your grade. However, after the class is over and your grades are officially released, then you can give the teacher a souvenir from your country or another sign of appreciation if you wish.

Employment

It is important to remember that your primary objective of coming to America is to study. Therefore, it is not advisable for you to take up any form of employment for the first semester. You should get settled, and once you have adjusted well, then you can seek employment either on- or off-campus. However, you must follow specific instructions and regulations as per your immigration status. Most importantly, you should not jeopardize your immigration status. Check with your international student services office regarding your eligibility to work and for help staying within legal guidelines.

Seeking Jobs

Almost all universities have an office on campus that posts job announcements on a bulletin board outside the office door or on their website. Another place to look is in the help wanted section that appears in the classified advertisement in the campus and city newspapers. You should always consult with other students for advice about employment. Students working on campus usually find jobs, such as maintaining grounds and buildings; guarding buildings at night; or working in cafeteria, library, or bookstore; cleaning homes of private individuals; and performing yard work and sometimes baby sitting duties (taking care of other people's children). Mostly for jobs related to your field of study, either on- or off-campus, the student services office or your specific department can help you.

Application Process

The first step in obtaining a job is to complete applications for individual employers. After you fill out the application, the organization may speak with you immediately or contact you for an interview later if you are one of the most qualified applicants. If you do not hear from the organization within two weeks, it is advisable to call back and find out whether you are going to be interviewed. When you get the interview, make sure you arrive a few minutes before the actual interview time. *Do not be late.* Make sure that you are well dressed and look your best. Be prepared to answer questions about your past job(s), qualifications, why you think you are the best person for the position, and why you want to work for that particular business or organization. You could further prepare yourself by getting the job description before the interview so that you know the exact job duties.

Social Security Taxes and Cards

Not all international students with an F-1 visa status have to pay Social Security taxes. Social Security is an American government program for people who retire at a certain age (65). The employer is required by law to take a small percentage out of each employee's wages to put into a national collection fund to pay for this program. Remember, to work in America, you must have a Social Security card (you can apply for one at the Social Security Administration in the city in which you live or by calling this office and requesting an application). On this card, you will see your full name and a unique nine-digit number known as your "Social Security Number," as stated by ISI.

State, Federal, and Income Taxes

You are required to pay state and federal taxes, which will be deducted automatically from your paycheck. However, whether you are required to pay income taxes depends on what tax agreements exist between America and your country. If your country does not have any agreement with America, you will be required to pay income taxes and to file a tax form the following year before April 15. You will have to complete both state and federal tax forms. On these forms, the record will show how much money you were paid on your job(s) during the previous year and how much money was deducted for both state and federal taxes. The payroll office of most universities will in most cases give you this vital information on a form called a W-2, which the employer must send to you (usually via mail) by January 31.

If your earnings were low for the previous year and taxes were withheld from your paychecks, the Internal Revenue Service (the agency with whom you file your federal tax return) and possibly your state revenue agency will return the excess money that was deducted from your paychecks. Various tax preparation businesses (i.e., H&R Block) should be located throughout your city. For a fee, the tax experts will prepare and file your taxes for you. In addition, some schools arrange for business students to help international students with their taxes. Both forms of tax returns can be filed manually (hardcopies are sent to the respective tax agencies) or electronically (prepared on the computer and submitted over the Internet). When your returns are filed electronically, your refund is sent to your bank account, but when your returns are filed manually, you will receive a paper check. The process takes about two to three weeks for electronic returns and two months or more for manually submitted returns.

Religion and Socialization
Right to Worship

According to the ISI, the constitution of America guarantees all residents the right to worship as they please. Within this right, the government cannot establish a national religion or give support to any church or sect (religious group). As long as you do not break any laws, you may worship as you would normally in your home country. There are churches, synagogues, mosques, or temples for various religions in most cities in America. At most universities, you will also find some on-campus religious organizations, which invite students to participate.

Making Friends

You can easily make friends or meet students in clubs, religious groups, international student organizations, student centers, and recreational buildings. You should not be afraid to start a conversation and should not allow one bad experience to discourage you. Americans often greet each other by saying "Hi" or "How are you?" However, this is not a request for information. It is a very informal American greeting. With some individuals, you will have no problem making conversation because they enjoy asking you many questions about life in your country. Others will seem shy or awkward around you because you are an international student. If you are having difficulty making conversation, ask the other people questions about their studies, family, or American life in general. In most cases, Americans will probably be happy to explain something you do not understand about classes or American social customs (also known as traditions).

Inappropriate Situations

In most cases, it is inappropriate to ask people about their age, the amount of money they earn, or the price they paid for an item. It is also inappropriate to ask a newly wedded woman if she is pregnant. Another area that you should avoid is making comments about how fat or big someone is. You should also be careful about approaching members of the opposite sex because they may misunderstand your intentions (ISI). What you see on American television or in the movies is not the norm for relationships between men and women. Most American men and women have learned to treat each other as equals, each deserving the same amount of respect and fair treatment in any situation.

Americans value honesty and they often say exactly what they think, even if it seems rude. For example, most Americans would prefer to hear "I am sorry, but I cannot come visit you tonight because I have to study," rather than to hear you will come and then not visit. In addition, Americans often have many acquaintances (people they have met and know by name) but few close friends. While Americans may seem friendly when you first meet, they may not be interested in a deeper relationship. Be very sensitive to others' expectations (ISI).

Dress Code

When it comes to dressing, Americans are very informal. For most social occasions, especially among university students, blue jeans or casual slacks are proper for both men and women. For some occasions, such as weddings, church services, or dinner in a nice restaurant, one needs semi-formal clothing (suits for men, dresses for women). If you are not sure of what to wear, please ask an American friend what would be appropriate for the occasion. If you are ever asked to do something that makes you feel uncomfortable, simply reply by saying "no thank you" or "I would rather not do that."

Timeliness

Americans are much more time-conscious than people from most other cultures. If you have an appointment with someone for 4:00pm, you are expected to be promptly on time or a few minutes early. This is true for any appointment or meeting, whether it is a business meeting or social event. In any event, make it a habit of calling the person with whom you are meeting to let him or her know that you are running late and at what time you expect to arrive. One exception is a casual party or "open house," in which case guests may arrive at any time after the events starts (ISI).

Informal Dinners

An informal dinner with a group of people is sometimes referred to as a *potluck*, which means that everyone brings food to share. Sometimes the host will ask you to bring a certain type of dish, such as a salad, special dish from your country, or dessert. The potluck could be a picnic, which is usually held at a park, or a barbecue, which is like a picnic except that the main meal is meat cooked on a grill. In most cases, you will be expected to bring your own meat, such as hamburgers, hot dogs, and chicken. When you are invited to someone's home for dinner, you may want to ask whether it is necessary for you to bring anything for the meal. For any invitation you receive, make sure you ask whether you can bring your children or other friends. Americans often host activities that are strictly by invitation and activities that do not include children. You may question whether you should bring a gift. The answer is usually no, unless it is an occasion such as a birthday, wedding, or graduation. Instead, you may send a "thank you" note or souvenir from your country to your host as a token of your appreciation. After the dinner, picnic, or barbecue, you should politely offer to help clean up or do the dishes. Often, your host will enjoy talking with you while you work together, and this is an informal way for your friend and you to get to know each other better (ISI).

Health Care and Insurance

America does not have a national medical care program that pays for all heath care. Since individuals are responsible for paying for their own medical expenses, which are usually very high, you have to buy health insurance to pay for your medical costs. At most universities, the international student services office offers a special insurance policy for international students. If you have insurance from your own country, you may need to find out whether you need additional insurance or whether what you have will be accepted.

Selecting a Health Plan

As with automobile insurance, when buying health insurance, you pay premiums based on the types of medical expenses that are covered under the policy in which you are enrolled. For example, some policies do not pay for routine examinations, dental or eye care, or the amount of your deductible. Under health insurance deductibles, you pay a certain amount of medical expenses, and the insurance company pays any expenses incurred throughout the year above that amount. Like automobile insurance, the higher your deductible, the lower your premiums will be (ISI).

Seeking Medical Care

Most universities have their medical center on campus. If you need medical care that the center cannot provide, the health center will recommend you to a physician or to a hospital in the city. If you so desire to have your own medical doctor, check in your telephone book's Yellow Pages (dentists are listed separately). Doctors are listed according to their specialty. If you are not sure who to select, please check with the health center, the international student services office, or an American friend, or call a physician referral services.

For a doctor's appointment, telephone your health center or the doctor's office during regular business hours, giving your name, the name of the doctor you want to see, and why. If you have an emergency, the doctor may see you that day, depending on the type of emergency. For injuries or illnesses that are serious but not life-threatening, first try to contact the doctor or clinic by telephone before going directly to the office. The clinic personnel will tell you what to do next. For life-threatening injuries or illnesses or for a serious medical emergency in which a person cannot or should not be moved, contact an ambulance by dialing 911.

Summary

As international students, when you leave home, you lose a familiar support system, especially Africans because generally, we depend so much on each other. Due to losing this support system, there is increased anxiety and loss of self-esteem. Though the adjustment process can affect individuals very differently, it is considered to be a difficult, reactive, and conflicting process rather than a smooth transition.

For African students, failure is not an option because to fail or to perform poorly might result in shame not only to the individuals involved, but also to their families. We cannot afford to fail because our families will be disappointed, and we do not want to see that happen. Therefore, if you carefully follow everything that I have discussed in this chapter, your transition will be less difficult, and your success will be guaranteed. This has been proven through the experiences of other who have come to study in the U.S.

Finally, the various universities say congratulations, and welcome. They are all pleased that you have chosen their university for furthering your education in America.

Chapter V. Overall Summary, Conclusion,

and Recommendations

With this book, I have attempted to contribute to the body of knowledge pertaining to the identification of adjustment problems of African students and international students in general. Recommendations will be offered for practitioners of international student services departments.

Overall Summary

As discussed previously, International students on the American college campus comprise a diverse and increasing population whose unique concerns are traditionally overlooked (Mori, 2000). The increase in pluralism and cultural diversity in the US has been markedly reflected in its educational systems (Institute of International Education, 2002). According to Thomas and Althen (1989), international students share certain characteristics regardless of their diverse cultural, social, religious, and political backgrounds. For instance, unlike other ethnic minorities, refugees, or recent immigrants, most international students plan to return to their home countries eventually and are in the US only temporarily. They are people in transition who choose to live in a foreign academic setting to realize their educational objectives. Because they are far away from their families, other relatives, and friends, they are also likely to have basic social support networks that are very distinctive from those of American students. Faced with a new set of basic values and beliefs, international students are continually challenged to accommodate themselves to a variety of acculturation and adjustment problems (Berry, 1980).

While international students have to deal with most of the concerns faced by all American students, they are confronted with a host of additional requirements that challenge even the most resilient students. Typically, international students have to adjust to drastically different foods, climates, educational systems, social values, and language (Verghese, 2002). Despite the fact that international students, as a group, have many important commonalties, the types of their acculturative stress, culture adjustment issues, and help-seeking behavior vary depending on factors such as ethnicity, gender, age, religious and linguistic backgrounds, sexual orientation, marital status, and area of residence in the US. Unfortunately, studies that focus on these factors are scarce in the literature.

Colleges and universities usually view foreign students as a source of diversity, enlightenment, and revenue. However, as already discussed, they also bring with them special needs. Kahne (1976) suggested that international student adjustment could be better understood when studied in the light of the academic and social contexts of the institution in which international students are enrolled. It is the responsibility of the institution to deal with these needs, starting when these students arrive on campus. Therefore, the rationale for this study was to provide data that might lead to better services for international students and better planning for effective international orientation programs. Therefore, and in general, there is a need to study the adjustment problems that all international students experience. More specifically, there is a paucity of information related to the adjustment of African students. Thus, this book also pinpoints how these different variables may affect the adjustment problems among African students.

Discussion of Findings

Acculturation and adjustment studies on international students have revealed that certain variables, such as perceived discrimination, less use of the English language, shorter time spent in the US, and religion are related to lower levels of acculturation and adjustment (Mori, 2000). Mori went on to further state that the English language barrier is probably the most significant, prevalent problem for the majority of international students. Many researchers (Greene, 1998; Hart, 1974; Maundeni, 1999; Mori, 2000; Nilson, 1997; Payind, 1977; Porter, 1962) have found that the English language was an important aspect of the international student's process of adjusting to the American culture. A study by Perkins, Mark, Gulielmo, and Reiff (1977), which compared the adjustment problems of three international groups, found that the English language was a major factor in the overall adjustment of international students studying in American universities and colleges. Those students who came from countries where the English language was taught in their schools were more likely to adjust faster (Pendar, 1987). Essandoh (1995) also found that international students who came to America with an understanding of the English language at the high school level adjusted much quicker. Previous research from the Michigan International Student Problem Inventory (Porter, 1962) revealed that international students who did not speak English as a first preference experienced more problems than those who spoke English as a first preference.

Contrary to the findings of Hart (1974), Han (1996), McCoy (1996), and Sharma (1973), but consistent with the findings of Arubayi (1980), Onyeanusi (1987), and Pendar (1987), African students studying at American colleges ranked English language as the least problematic concern. This conclusion is consistent with the findings of a study that I conducted on African students at Western Michigan University, whereby the students rated the English language as their problem of least concern.

A study of age findings (Arubayi, 1980) compared the adjustment problems among different age groups and found that the younger students (age 20 and below) reported significantly more problems in only one problem area, namely the English language. This is contrary to the findings of some studies, as mentioned above. Another study found that international students 32 years or older reported significantly more problems than students 22–25 years or younger.

My study (Goyol, 2002) found that African students reported having problems with immigration work restrictions. These results support, in part, the research findings of a number of studies on international students in America (Breuder, 1972; Essandoh, 1995; Hart, 1974; Hill, 1966; Pendar, 1987; Santos, 1959; Sharma, 1973). Essandoh (1995), who surveyed a group of African students, found finances to be among their major concerns. The financial situation for most African students has been compounded by the restrictions placed on working by the US INS and the poor economic situation in most African countries, whereby education budgets are not large enough to sponsor students abroad because there are so many other services that are competing for the limited resources.

In the social–personal area (Goyol, 2002), I found that African students have problems dealing with the attitudes of some Americans regarding skin color, homesickness, and trying to make friends. The results support, in part, the research findings of Arubayi (1980) and Essandoh (1995), both of whom reported that the most frequent problems African students experience is the attitudes some people have relating to skin color. In addition, 50% of the students reported having problems with changes in weather conditions, which can be understood in view of the warmer climate in Africa. Arubayi (1980), Essandoh (1995), and Pendar (1987), who conducted research related to the adjustment problems of African students, found that changes in weather in the Midwestern region were a problem.

Finally, it could also be assumed that African students at public universities in America are not overly stressed due to their good English language background, good orientation program, and good support network from other African students on the various campuses.

Conclusion and Recommendations

The purpose of this book is to identify the adjustment problems experienced by African students studying in public universities in America. Hopefully, the book has helped answer some questions pertaining to adjustment and acculturation problems encountered by African students studying in America. Since this book is restricted primarily to African students, the validity of the findings is limited to this student population only. For greater generalization, further investigation should be conducted with all international students throughout the US for comparison purposes to confirm or reject the conclusions of this book.

Policy

As presented in this book, researchers have found that financial issues seemed to be the most prevalent problems encountered by African students at public universities in America. Among the problem situations that students reported as of "concern" or "most concern" were: immigration work restrictions and lack of money to meet expenses. Therefore, to help the students manage their financial difficulties, the Economic Hardship Policy (INS, News Release, 1998) should be extended to African students. According to the policy, if an unfortunate situation arises that affects an F-1 student's financial status at Western Michigan University, a student may be eligible to apply for work authorization based on severe economic hardship. In June 1998, the INS, in response to the current economic crises in Asia, announced that it was temporarily lifting certain employment restrictions for F-1 student visa holders whose means of financial support come from Indonesia, Malaysia, the Philippines, South Korea, and Thailand. This change was aimed at helping eligible students afford to continue their studies. The currencies of the five aforementioned countries had recently plummeted in value relative to the US dollar, causing severe economic hardships for many of the estimated 80,000 students currently enrolled in US colleges and universities whose financial support is derived from these countries. However, African countries also have a history of economic hardship and political instability. Therefore, African nations should be included in the countries that benefit from such a policy.

Secondly, due to my findings, I propose that technical cooperation could be entered into between public universities with African students and their various home countries, giving opportunity to some of the faculty and students of American universities, which can enable them to experience first-hand contact with each other's cultures. Eventually, this will result in a better understanding between the US and other countries.

Thirdly, orientation programs have become a huge contributing factor to the adjustment process of African students to public universities in America. Therefore, it is important that the various international student services offices in charge of organizing these programs ensure that leaders of the programs help prepare African students for the values and social practices that shape the ways Americans relate to others in general. This in turn may give African students a more realistic picture of what to expect at their various universities. It is recommended that after every orientation program, an internal appraisal of the program should be conducted to get immediate feedback about identifying problems and coming up with ways constantly to improve the program.

Fourthly, I strongly recommend development of a mentor–mentee system that would help African students with integration into the American academia. It is important for all students to create a bond with someone who has insight into their program(s) of choice. This way, if these students ever get off track in their studies, they have someone to turn to for assistance.

Fifthly, a log should be kept in the office of international student services to document problems and concerns of the students. At the end of each semester, any visits made by international students to this office should be properly documented. The information could then be used to identify problems areas for these students, which will then be used to enhance new and effective ways to better serve the students.

The theory of acculturation focuses on understanding the adaptation processes and cultural changes of minority groups as they experience first-hand contact with a dominant culture (Sodowsky & Plake, 1992; Sodowsky et al, 1991). Differences that distinguish one culture from others are what provide individuals of the first culture with a unique sense of cultural identity—they are impossible to replicate in a foreign country. The loss of cultural objects, such as the symbolism of the national flag, music and art, as well as numerous other background aspects of the home culture, can have a significant impact on the international student's quality of adjustment in the new environment. Therefore, a thorough understanding of the problems faced by these students should lead to more successful ways of dealing with such issues, allowing the students themselves to make their own adjustments.

Research

In order to obtain more comprehensive information concerning the problems that African students experience in the US, a comparative investigation should be conducted between these students and other international students enrolled in colleges and universities across the US. Most research on acculturation and adjustment of international students has used quantitative methods. Therefore, it is recommended that a mixed approach be considered. Qualitative interviewing may provide a means of enriching quantitative data (Lincoln & Guba, 1985; Patton, 1990). Furthermore, a longitudinal study would enable a direct test of the curvilinear pattern of acculturation and adjustment (i.e., repeated measurement of international students as they progress each year they are studying in the US).

Finally, you have all come a long way. Your ultimate goal of coming to America is academics. Therefore, the primary objective of this book has been to present you with realistic and practical information that will make your academic venture to America a successful and memorable experience. I sincerely believe that many of you are highly motivated for yourselves, your families, and the prestige to achieve academically at an American university. The potential impact of your studying in this country cannot be quantified. It can only be best imagined. Among you will be political leaders, scientists, researchers, or in a nut shell, the intellectual strength of many countries in the African continent. Therefore, the knowledge and experience you get will have enormous implications that will invariably contribute to economic, social, educational, and political growth. Again, congratulations, and welcome to your various campuses.

Bibliography

Adelegan, F. O., and D. J. Parks. "Problems of Transition for African Students in an American University." *Journal of College Student Personnel* 26 (1985): 504-8.

Akpan-Iquot, E. D. "An Investigation of Foreign Students' Problems in Selected Oklahoma Institutions of Higher Learning (Doctoral Dissertation, Oklahoma State University, 1980)." *Dissertation Abstracts International* 42 (1981): 95-A (University Microfilms No. 81-13290).

Alsaffer, A. A. "A Survey of International Students' Opinions and Attitudes at the University of Tennessee (1976)." *Dissertation Abstracts International* 37 (1977): 6851-A (University Microfilms No. 77-10751).

Altscher, D. C. "A Rationale for Counseling Program Designed Uniquely for International Students." Paper presented at the Annual Convention of the American Personnel and Guidance Association, Chicago, Illinois (ERIC Document Reproduction Service, No. 77-10751).

Arjona, A. Q. "An Experiential Study of the Adjustment Problems of a Group of Foreign Graduate Students and a Group of American Graduate Students at Indiana University (Doctoral Dissertation, Indiana University, 1956)." *Dissertation Abstracts International* 16 (1956): 1838 (University Microfilms No. 56-1757).

Arubayi, E. A. "Identification of Problems Experienced by Nigerian Students Enrolled in Kansas State University." (1980) (ERIC Document Reproduction Service No. ED 198 424).

—. "Perceptions of Problems Identified by Nigerian Students in American Higher Institutions: A Comparative Analysis." *College Student Journal* 15, no. 2 (1981): 116-120.

Beck, A. T., and J. E. Young. "College Blues." *Psychology Today* 12, no. 4 (1978): 80-92.

Becker, T. "Patterns of Attitudinal Changes among Foreign Students." *American Journal of Sociology* 73 (1968): 431-42.

Beeve, G. A. *The Foreign Student in the New York City Area.* New York: Greater New York Council for Foreign Students, 1955.

Berry, J. W. "Accultural as Varieties of Adaptation." Pp. 9-25 in *Accultural: Theory, Models and Some New Findings*, edited by A.M. Boulder, & Co.: Westview Press, 1980.

—. "Acculturation: A Comparative Analysis of Alternative Forms." Pp. 65-78 in *Perspectives in Immigration and Minority Education*, edited by R.J. Samuda and S.L. Woods. New York: University Press of America, 1983.

Berry, J. W., U. Kim, T. Minde, and D. Mok. "Comparative Studies of Acculturative Stress." *International Migration Review* 21 (1987): 491-511.

Bradley, L., G. Parr, W. Y. Lan, R. Bingi, and L. J. Gould. "Counseling Expectations of International Students." *International Journal for the Advancement of Counseling* 18 (1995): 21-31.

Breuder, R. L. *A Statewide Study: Identified Problems of International Students Enrolled in Public Community/Junior Colleges in Florida*. Tallahassee, FL: The Florida State University, Department of Higher Education, 1972 (ERIC Document Reproduction Service No. ED 062 977).

Bulthuis, . "The Foreign Student Today: A Profile." *New Directions for Students Services* 36 (1986): 19-27.

Cable, J. N. "Foreign Students in the United States." *Improving College and University Teaching* 22, no. 1 (1974): 40-41.

Carey, P., and M. Alemayehu. "Minoritization: Toward an Explanatory Theory of Foreign Student Adjustment in the United States." *Negro Educational Review* 31, nos. 3-4 (1980): 127-136.

Cheng, D., F. T. Leong, and R. Geist. "Cultural Differences in Psychological Distress between Asian and Caucasian American College Students." *Journal of Multicultural Counseling and Development* 21, no. 3 (1993): 182-190.

Clapper, T. H. "Teaching American Government to Foreign Students." *Teaching Political Science* 3, no. 3 (1976): 311-16.

Coan, C. *The International Campus*. Lawrence, Ks.: Kansas University, 1971 (ERIC Document Reproduction Service No. ED 066 135).

Connolly, J. J. "International Students and the Two-Year College." *Junior College Journal* 37 (1967): 20-21.

Cormack, M. L. *An Evaluation of Research on Educational Exchange*. New York: Brooklyn College, 1962.

Das, A. K., S. Y. Chow, and B. Rutherford. "The Counseling Needs of Foreign Students." *International Journal for the Advancement of Counseling* 9 (1986): 167-74.

Davis, T. M., ed. *Open Doors 1995/96: Report on International Educational Exchange*. New York: Institute of International Education, 1996.

Day, R. C., and F. M. Hajj. "Delivering Counseling Services to International Students: The Experience of the American University of Beirut." *Journal of College Student Personnel* 7 (1986): 353-57.

Deutsch, S. R. *International Aspects of Higher Education Exchange: A Community Study*. Cleveland, Oh.: Western Reserve University, 1965 (ERIC Document Reproduction Service No. ED 010 552).

DuBois, C. *Foreign Students and Higher Education in the United States*. Washington, DC: American Council Education, 1956.

Eddy, M. S. *Foreign Students in the United States: Is the Welcome Mat Out?* Washington, DC: National Institution of Education (DHEW), 1978 (ERIC Document Reproduction Service No. ED 165 524).

Essandoh, P. K. "Counseling Issues with African College Students in U.S. Colleges and Universities." *The Counseling Psychologist* 23, no. 2 (1995): 348-60.

Forstat, E. R. "Adjustment Problems of International Students." *Sociology and Social Research* 36, no. 1 (1951): 25-30.

Gabriel, R. L. "Characteristics of Foreign Students on an American Campus." *Journal of the National Association of Women Deans and Counselors* 36, no. 4 (1972): 184.

Galvan, J. L. *Writing Literature Reviews: A Guide for Students of the Social and Behavioral Sciences.* Los Angeles: Pyrczak Publishing, 1999.

Georgiades, J. G. "Identified Problems of International Students: Public New Jersey Community Colleges and Rutgers - The State University of New Jersey (Doctoral Dissertation, Rutgers University, The State University of New Jersey, 1980)." *Dissertation Abstracts International* 41 (1981): 3900-901-A (University Microfilms No. 81-05221).

Ginter, E. J., and A. Glauser. *A Developmental Life Skills Model: A Comprehensive Approach for Students.* Presentation made at the 22nd Annual University System of Georgia's Learning Support/Development Studies Conference, Augusta, Ga., (April 1997).

Graves, T. "Psychological Acculturation in a Tri-Ethnic Community." *Southwestern Journal* 23 (1967): 337-50.

Green, S. B., N. L. Salkind, and T. M. Akey. *Using SPSS for Windows: Analysis and Understanding Data.* 2nd ed. Upper Saddle River, NJ: Prentice Hall, 2000.

Greene, A. "Adjustment Problems Perceived by Taiwanese, Korean, and Japanese International Students at California State University, Fullerton." Unpublished PhD Dissertation, California State University, Fullerton, Ca., 1998.

Goyol, A. B. "Adjustment Problems of African Students at Western Michigan University." Unpublished PhD Dissertation, Western Michigan University, Kalamazoo, Mi., 2002.

Gullahorn, J. T., and J. E. Gullahorn. "An Extension of the U-Curve Hypothesis." *Journal of Social Issues* 19, no. 3 (1963): 33-47.

Hamboyan, H., and A. K. Bryan. "International Students: Culture Shock Can Affect the Health of Students from Abroad." *Canadian Family Physician* 41 (1995): 1713-16.

Han, H. Y. "A Study of the Adjustment Problems of Korean Students in the Pittsburgh Area." PhD Dissertation, University of Pittsburgh, Pittsburgh, Pa., 1996.

Hart, R. H. "Problems of International Students Enrolled in Texas Public Colleges as Perceived by International Student Advisors." Paper presented at the 1981 Central Region Seminar of the Association of Community College Trustees, "Community Colleges—Lifeboats for the Future", Osage Beach, Mo. (ERIC Document Reproduction Service No. ED 206 359), April 12-14, 1981.

—. "Problems of International Students Enrolled in Texas Public Colleges as Perceived by International Student Advisors (Doctoral Dissertation, East Texas State University, 1974)." *Dissertation Abstracts* 35 (1974): 2683-A (University Microfilms No. 74-25632).

Hayes, R. L. and H-R. Lin. "Coming to America: Developing Social Support Systems for International Students." *Journal of Multicultural Counseling and Development* 22 (1994): 7-16.

Heath, D. "Foreign Student Attitudes at the International House." *Berkeley International, Education, and Cultural Exchange* 53 (1970): 66-70.

Heikinheimo, P. S., and J. C. Shute. "The Adaptation of Foreign Students: Students Views and Institutional Implications." *Journal of College Student Personnel* 9 (1986): 399-406.

Hill, J. H. "An Analysis of a Group of Indonesian, Thai, Pakistani, and Indian Students' Perceptions of Their Problems While Enrolled at Indiana University (Doctoral Dissertation, Indiana University, 1966)." *Dissertation Abstracts,* 27 (1966): 2007 (University Microfilms No. 66-12657).

Hopp, J. W. "Specialized Field Work for International Health Education Students: A Survey of Need." *The Journal of School Health* 47, no. 8 (1996): 481-2.

Howard, J. M., and R. Keele. "International Students in a U.S. Graduate Business Program: Cultures, Subcultures, and the New Student." Paper presented at the Annual Eastern Michigan University Conference on Languages and Communication for World Business and the Professions, Ypsilanti, Mi. (ERIC Document Reproduction Services No. ED 246 770) April 3-5, 1991.

How to Survive in the U.S.: A Handbook of Internationals: International Student, Inc., 1995. Office of International Students and Scholars. "Orientation for Yale International Students. 2004. <http://www.oiss.yale.edu/student/ois.htm> (6 June 2004).

Huang, K. "Campus Mental Health: The Foreigner at Your Desk." *The Journal of the American College Health Association* 25 (1977): 216-19.

. *Open Doors 1993/1994: Report on International Education Exchange.* New York: Institute of International Education, 1994.

Institute of International Education. "Foreign Student by Academic Level and Place of Origin (2000/01)." 2002. <http:www.opendoorsweb.org/2001%20Files/ 2Table_edited.htm> .

ISORP News. "International Student Orientation and Registration Program." 2004. <http://www.wmich.edu/oiss> (6 June 2004).

Jarrahi-Zadeh, A., and W. J. Eichman. "The Impact of Sociocultural Factors on Middle-Eastern Students in the U.S." *International Educational and Cultural Exchange* 5 (1970): 82-94.

Johnson, D. C. "Problems of Foreign Students." *International Educational and Cultural Exchange* 7, no. 2 (1971): 61-8.

Kahne, M. J. "Cultural Differences: Whose Troubles are We Talking About?" *International Educational and Cultural Exchange* 11, no. 4 (1973): 36-40.

Kao, C. C. "Adjustment Problems Perceived by Chinese Students Attending Universities in the Metropolitan Washington, D.C. Area." EdD Dissertation, Catholic University of America, 1987.

Klein, M. H., et al. "The Foreign Student Adaptation Program: Social Experiences of Asian Students in the U.S." *International Educational and Cultural Exchange* 6, no. 3 (1971): 77-90.

Knapp, A. E., and M. Whitmore. "Bridging Cultural Gaps: A Workshop for International Students." Pittsburgh: University of Pittsburgh, 1991 (ERIC Document Reproduction Service No. ED 345 638).

Kurtz, I. G. "International Education in Pluralistic Society." (1981):

Lee, A. R. "Culture Shift and Popular Protest in South Korea." *Comparative Political Studies* 26, no. 1 (1993): 63-80.

Leong, F. T., and W. E. Sedlacek. "Academic and Career Needs of International Students and United States College Students." *Journal of College Development* 30 (1989): 106-111.

Lincoln, U. S., and E. G. Guba. *Naturalistic Inquiry.* Newbury Park, Ca.: Sage, 1985.

Livingstone, A. S. *The Overseas Student in Britain.* Manchester, England: Manchester University Press, 1960.

Lonner, W. and F. Ibrahim. "Research about Effectiveness." In P. Pedersen, J. W. Draguns, and J. Timble (Eds), Counseling across cultures (4th ed). Thousand Oaks, Ca.: Sage, 1996.

Lysgaard, S. "Adjustment in a Foreign Society: Norwegian Fulbright Grantees Visiting the United States." *International Social Science Bulletin* 7, no. 1 (1955): 45-51.

Mantakara, K. "Attitudes and Opinions of Thai Students in the United States: An Analysis (Doctoral Dissertation, Boston College, 1975)." *Dissertation Abstracts International* (1975): 1219-A (University Microfilms No. 75-20705).

Maxwell, M. J. "Foreign Students and American Academic Ritual." *Journal of Reading* 17, no. 4 (1974): 301-5.

Maundeni, T. "African Females and Adjustment to Studying Abroad." *Gender & Education* 11(1) (1999).

McCoy, M. A. "A Study of the Self-Perceived Problems among Asian Students at the University of Memphis." EdD Dissertation, University of Memphis, Memphis, Tn., 1996.

McGoldrick, M., J. Giordano, and J. K. Peardce, eds. *Ethnicity and Family Therapy.* 2nd ed. New York: The Guilford Press, 1996.

Meyer, C. R. "A Survey of the Concerns of International Students at Texas Woman's University in Relation to Selected Student Personnel Services." Master of Arts Thesis. College of Education, Texas Woman's University, Tx., 1984.

Moravcsik, M. J. "Foreign Students in the Natural Sciences: A Growing Challenge." *International Educational and Cultural Exchange* 9, no. 1 (1973): 45-57.

Mori, S. "Addressing the Mental Health Concerns of International Students." *Journal of Counseling & Development* 2 (2000): 137-44.

Moyerman, D. R., and B. D. Forman. "Acculturation and Adjustment: A Meta-Analytic Study." *Hispanic Journal of Behavioral Science* 14, no. 2 (1992): 163-200.

Nilson, J. "Gender Differences in Acculturation: A Qualitative Study of International Students." Unpublished research. Western Michigan University, Kalamazoo, Mi., 1997.

Nunnaly, J. C. *Psychometric Theory.* New York: McGraw-Hill, 1978.

Onyeanusi, O. E. "A Comparison of Adjustment Problems to American Higher Education Perceived by Nigerian and Other International Students at Selected Universities in the Philadelphia Area with Implications for Vocational Education Students in Nigeria." EdD Dissertation, Temple University, 1987.

Othman, A. H. "The Identification of Adjustment Problems, Life Change Stress and Perceived Usefulness of Problem-Solving Resources in a Malay Student Sample in the United States (Doctoral Dissertation, Indiana University, 1979)." *Dissertation Abstracts International* 40 (1980): 3788-A (University Microfilms No. 80-00646).

Ozbay, Y. "An Investigation of the Relationship between Adaptational Coping Processes and Self-Perceived Negative Feelings on International Students." *Dissertation Abstracts International* 54 (1984): 2958-A.

Patten, M. L. *Proposing Empirical Research: A Guide to the Fundamentals.* Los Angeles: Pyrczak, 2000.

Patton, M. Q. *Qualitative Evaluation and Research Methods.* Newbury Park, Ca.: Sage, 1990.

Parker, O. D. "Cultural Clues to the Middle Eastern Student." *International Educational and Cultural Exchange* 12, no. 2 (1972): 12-18.

Payind, M. A. "Academic, Personal and Social Problems of Afgan and Iranian Students in the United States (Doctoral Dissertation, Indiana University, 1977)." *Dissertation Abstracts International* 38 (1977): 4613-A (University Microfilms No. 77 30312).

Pedersen, P. B. "Counseling International Students." *Counseling Psychologist* 19 (1991): 10-58.

Pendar, J. N. "Selected Adjustment Problems of Cameroonian Students Pursuing Higher Education in the San Francisco Bay Area of Northern California." EdD Dissertation, School of Education, University of San Francisco, San Francisco, Ca., 1987.

Pender, P. B. "Counseling International Students." *The Counseling Psychologist* 19, no. 1 (1991): 10-58.

Perkins, C. S., M. L. Perkins, L. M. Guglielmino, and R. F. Reiff. "A Comparison of the Adjustment Problems of Three International Student Groups." *Journal of College Student Personnel* 18, no. 5 (1977): 382-8.

Peterson, J. A., and M. H. Neumeyer. "Problems of Foreign Students." *Sociology and Social Research* 32 (1948): 787-92.

Porter, J. W. "The Development of an Inventory to Determine the Problems of Foreign Students." PhD Dissertation, Michigan State University, Mi., 1962.

Pruitt, F. J. "The Adaptation of Foreign Students on American Campuses." *Journal of the Administrators and Counselors* 41, no. 41 (1978): 144-47.

Redfield, R., R. Linton, and M. T. Herskovits. "Memorandum for the Study of Acculturation." *American Anthropologist* 38 (1936): 149-52.

Robinson, T. L., and E. J. Ginter, eds. "Racism: Healing Its Effects." *Journal of Counseling Development* (special issue) 77, no. 1 (1999).

Saleh, M. A. "The Personal, Social, and Academic Adjustment Problems of Arab Students at Selected Texas Institutions of Higher Education (Doctoral Dissertation, North Texas State University, 1979)." *Dissertation Abstracts International* 40 (1980): 6168-A (University Microfilms No. 80-12874).

Salim, S. "Adjustment Problems of Malaysian Students at Western Michigan University (Doctoral Dissertation, Western Michigan University, 1984)." *Dissertation Abstracts International* (1984): 9999.2 .S24x.

Sandhu, D. S. "An Examination of the Psychological Needs of the International Student: Implications for Counseling and Psychotherapy." *International Journal of the Advancement of Counseling* 17 (1995): 229-39.

Sandhu, D. S., & B. R. Asrabadi. "Development of an Acculturative Stress Scale for International Students: Preliminary Findings." *Psychological Reports* 75 (1994): 435-48.

Santos, A. P. "A Study of the Problems Faced by Foreign Students at Indiana University with Implications for Action (Doctoral Dissertation, Indiana University, 1959)." *Dissertation Abstracts International* 20 (1959): 3580 (University Microfilms No. 59-6587).

Sasnett, M. T. "Foreign Students Problems on American Campuses." *College and University* 26 (1950): 93-101.

Scott, F. D. *The American Experience of Swedish Students*. Minneapolis, Min.: University of Minnesota Press, 1956.

Selby, H., and C. Woods. "Foreign Students at a High-Pressure University." *Sociology of Education* 39 (1966): 138-54.

Sewell, W. II., and O. M. Davidson. "The Adjustment of Scandinavian Students." *Journal of Social Issues* 12, no. 1 (1956): 9-19.

Shannon, D. M., and M. A. Daveport. *Using SPSS to Solve Statistical Problems*. Columbus, Oh.: Merrill Prentice Hall, 2000.

Sharma, S. "A Study to Identify and Analyze Adjustment Problems Experienced by Foreign Non-European Graduate Students Enrolled in Selected Universities in the State of North Carolina." *California Journal of Educational Research* 24, no. 3 (1973): 135-46.

Smith, M. B. "Some Features of Foreign Student Adjustment." *Journal of Higher Education* 16, no. 5 (1955): 231-41.

Sodowsky, G. R., E. W. Lai, and B. S. Plake. "Moderating Effects of Socio-Cultural Variable on Acculturation Attitudes of Hispanics and Asian–Americans." *Journal of Counseling & Development* 70 (1991): 194-204.

Sodowsky, G. R., and B. S. Plake. "A Study of Acculturation Differences among International People and Suggestions for Sensitivity to Within-

Group Differences." *Journal of Counseling & Development* 71 (1992): 53-59.

Spaulding, S., and M. J. Flack. *The World's Students in United States: A Review and Evaluation of Research on Foreign Students.* New York: Praeger Publishers, 1976.

Spradley, J. P., and M. Phillips. "Culture and Stress: A Quantitative Analysis." *American Anthropologist* 74 (1972): 518-29.

Surdam, J. C., and J. R. Collins. "Adaptation of International Students: A Cause for Concern." *Journal of College Student Personnel* 25 (1984): 240-45.

Strang, R. M. *Behavior and Backgrounds of Students in Colleges and Secondary Schools.* New York: Harper and Brothers, 1937.

Sundberg, N. D. "Toward Research Evaluating Intercultural Counseling." *Counseling Across Cultures*, edited by P. Pederson, W. J. Lonner, and J. G. Draguns. Honolulu, Haw.: The University Press of Hawaii, 1977.

South Korea: A New Society." *The Economist* 311 (1987): 23-24, 26.

Swanson, J. B. "Traditional Programs Fall Short." *The Agricultural Education Magazine* 52, no. 1 (1973): 5, 8.

Tabachnick, B. G., and L. S. Fidell. *Using Multivariate Statistics.* 2nd ed. New York: Harper Collins Publisher, 1988.

Thomas, K., and G. Althen. "Counseling Foreign Students." Pp. 205-41 in *Counseling Across Cultures*, edited by P. B. Pedersen, J. G. Draguns, W. J. Lonner, and J. E. Trimble. 3rd ed. Honolulu, Haw.: University of Hawaii Press, 1989.

Verghese, C. "Working with International Students: Cross Cultural and Psychodynamic Perspective." <http://www.acpa.nche.edu/comms/comm07/intlstudents.html> 2002.

Westwood, M. J., W. S. Lawrence, and D. Paul. "Preparing for Reentry: A Program for the Sojourning Student." *International Journal for the Advancement of Counseling* 9 (1986): 221-30.

Wilson, R. W. "Wellsprings of Discontent: Sources of Dissent in South Korean Student Values." *Asian Survey* 28, no. 10 (1987): 1066-81.

Win, U. K. "A Study of the Difficulties Indian and Japanese Students Encountered in Six Problem Areas at the University of Southern California (1969-1970)." *Dissertation Abstracts International* 33 (1971): 912-A (University Microfilms No. 72, 23 155).

Winchester, E. A., and Gilbertson, J. P. *Foreign Students in Washington's Colleges and Universities.* Olympia, WA: Washington State Council on Higher Education, 1972 (ERIC Document Reproduction Service No. ED 080 059).

Winkelman, M. "Cultural Shock and Adaptation." *Journal of Counseling & Development* 73 (1994): 121-26.

Wright, D. J. "Minority Students: Developmental Beginnings." *New Directions for Student Services* 38 (1987): 5-21.

Xia, Z. H. "Asian Students' Adjustment Problems at the University of Wisconsin-Madison." PhD Dissertation, Graduate School, University of Wisconsin-Madison, 1989.

Zain, E. K. "A Study of the Academic and Personal-Social Difficulties Encountered by a Select Group of Foreign Students at the University of Oregon (Doctoral Dissertation, University of Oregon, 1965)." *Dissertation Abstracts,* 26 (1966): 4352 (University Microfilms No. 65-12252).

Author Biographical Sketch

NAME	POSITION TITLE
Apollos B. Goyol	Assistant Professor and Evaluator

EDUCATION/TRAINING

INSTITUTION AND LOCATION	DEGREE	YEAR(s)	FIELD OF STUDY
Western Michigan University Kalamazoo, MI	BS	1989	Automotive Engineering
Western Michigan University Kalamazoo, MI	MA	1990	Vocational and Technical Education
Western Michigan University Kalamazoo, MI	PhD	2002	Evaluation, Measurement, and Research

PROFESSIONAL EXPERIENCE:

5/03—present: Assistant Professor and Evaluator, University of Arkansas for Medical Sciences, Office of Educational Development, Little Rock, AR.

10/95—04/03: Director for Planning and Implementation, Alternative Trade Network of Nigeria.

04/93—07/97: Head of the Department of Mechanical and Electrical Technology, Plateau State Polytechnic, Plateau State.

09/84—04/93: Senior Lecturer, Department of Mechanical and Electrical Technology, Plateau State Polytechnic, Plateau State.

COMMITTEES:

Plateau State Polytechnic Departmental Examination and Malpractice Committee, 1993-1997

University of Arkansas for Medical Sciences Faculty Development & Community Outreach, 2003—present

Western Michigan University Graduate Student Advisory Committee, 2002

Student Advisory Board, Western Michigan University College of Education, 2000—2002

Board of Directors, Western Michigan University Western Herald Newspaper, 2000—2002

MEMBERSHIPS:

American Educational Research Association, 2003

Michigan Association for Evaluation, 2002—present

American Evaluation Association, 1998—present

Editor Biographical Sketch

NAME	POSITION TITLE
Sheila K. Dodson	Writer/Editor

EDUCATION/TRAINING

INSTITUTION AND LOCATION	DEGREE	YEAR(s)	FIELD OF STUDY
University of Arkansas at Little Rock	BA	2001	Professional & Technical Writing
University of Arkansas at Little Rock	MA	2003	Professional & Technical Writing

PROFESSIONAL EXPERIENCE:

08/01—08/04:   Grant & Science Writer/Editor, University of Arkansas for Medical Sciences, Office of Grants & Scientific Publications, Little Rock, AR.

09/00—08/01:   Claims Adjudicator I, Arkansas Disability Determination for Social Security Administration, Little Rock, AR.

11/98—09/00:   Health Care Analyst II, Arkansas Department of Human Services, Division of Medical Services, Little Rock, AR.

07/97—11/98:   Family Support Specialist I, Arkansas Department of Human Services, Division of County Operations, North Little Rock, AR.

06/97—01/98:   Freelance Technical Writer, University of Arkansas for Medical Sciences, Little Rock, AR.

05/97—06/97:   Technical Writer/Editor, Manpower, Inc (Air Transport International), Little Rock, AR.

03/96—04/97:   Unlicensed Care Associate, Baptist Health Systems (Baptist Medical Center), Little Rock, AR.

02/95—03/96:   Technical Writer/Editor, Manpower, Inc (ALLTEL Information Services, formerly Systemati), Little Rock, AR.

Index